DON'T CALL THEM
Trailer Trash

The Illustrated Mobile Home Story

John Brunkowski & Michael Closen

DON'T CALL THEM Trailer Trash

Schiffer Publishing Ltd
4880 Lower Valley Road • Atglen, PA 19310

To our mothers
Bernice and Dorothy.

Library of Congress Control Number: 2016957637

Cover & Interior designed By Matt Goodman

Type set in ITC Franklin Gothic Std, Ed Roman

ISBN: 978-0-7643-5233-1

Printed in China

Published by Schiffer Publishing, Ltd.
4880 Lower Valley Road
Atglen, PA 19310
Phone: (610) 593-1777; Fax: (610) 593-2002
E-mail: Info@schifferbooks.com
Web: www.schifferbooks.com

For our complete selection of fine books on this and related subjects, please visit our website at www.schifferbooks.com. You may also write for a free catalog.

Schiffer Publishing's titles are available at special discounts for bulk purchases for sales promotions or premiums. Special editions, including personalized covers, corporate imprints, and excerpts, can be created in large quantities for special needs. For more information, contact the publisher.

We are always looking for people to write books on new and related subjects. If you have an idea for a book, please contact us at proposals@schifferbooks.com.

Contents

Mobile Home Manual

Paperback book by Trail-R-Club of America, 5.5" x 8.5", 197 pages, copyright 1954. The book variously called itself: *The Mobile Home How to Do IT Book* and *A Reference Book for All Mobile Home Owners.* We love the cover graphic of the upscale, futuristic, and very lengthy coach sporting a raised living room entrance area. $25-$30

A fun, classic image of the "trailer trash" stereotype. Advertising cardboard poster, by Hallmark, 14" x 12.25", c. 2010s. We found this wonderful piece at a Florida flea market and could not believe our good fortune. The picture of this little trailer house with its miniature white picket fence contains a number of other elements contributing to the stereotype, such as the lady in her housecoat and slippers, the shirtless fellow—both of them waving and drawing attention to themselves—the faux leopard skin door panel, and the plastic animal yard ornament. $5–$10

Introduction

This book is the first ever to tackle and challenge the "trailer trash" stereotype that has become ingrained in so many Americana images. This entertaining, informative, and fun book will set the record straight—or at least straighten it out a bit—about mobile homes and mobile-home living. After nearly a century of suffering the indignation of those fond of taunting trailer trash, the owners of mobile homes can finally lift their heads and go forth with the well-deserved pride of home ownership.

How did the trailer trash label get its start, and why has it steadfastly lasted so long? No one knows exactly when it first happened, but we do know how the process took place that added trailer trash to our lexicon. Most surely, the phrase resulted from a combination of unfortunate and exaggerated influences.

Everyone living outside the generally perceived norm is subject to doubt and even ridicule. There is a kind of counterculture of those living in mobile homes and trailer parks—as the choice to reside in the confines of a relatively small box, and especially in a cluster of similarly situated small boxes, is way out of the ordinary for the vast majority of normal folks. This novelty and difference has served as the biggest factor of all, causing people in general, and humorists in particular, to poke fun at mobile homes and their inhabitants. Thus, as the long development process began and progressed leading ultimately to the creation of the first true mobile homes, humorous criticism was directed at every stage in the process.

Doubters initially questioned ancient nomadic peoples who moved their makeshift huts from place to place; doubters laughed when the invention of the wheel led to its attachment to gypsy wagons, circus wagons, and covered wagons, allowing people to ride and live in moving horse-drawn vehicles; and doubters denigrated those who dared to affix primitive living quarters to equally primitive trailer chassis to be towed behind the newfangled automobiles of the early 1900s.

"Mobile Homes"

Collector educational information card (part of a large set about "Life In America"), black-and-white photo (c. 1940s), by Grolier Inc., #92-6, 6" x 4.5", with rounded corners, copyright 1998. This card referred to mobile homes as "factory-made, movable houses . . . Mobile homes developed from recreational camping vehicles . . . During World War II, the government used thousands of trailers as housing for soldiers and workers. After the war, a housing shortage increased the demand for mobile homes." According to the card, "An estimated 11 million Americans live in mobile homes; about half are located in the South." Scarce card! $15–$20

The Saturday Evening
POST
August 2, 1952 – 15¢

DON'T CALL THEM TRAILER TRASH

By HAROLD H. MARTIN

If you pity families who raise kids in house trailers—don't. Their dwelling may have cost more than yours, it's just as convenient, and a lot less trouble. Here's how these happy gypsies live.

"Don't Call Them Trailer Trash"

Magazine article, *Saturday Evening Post,* August 2, 1952, page 24. The tagline for this thoughtful and thorough piece reads: "If you pity families who raise kids in house trailers—don't. Their dwelling may have cost more than yours, it's just as convenient, and a lot less trouble. Here's how these happy gypsies live." This piece was an early attempt by an authoritative and highly acclaimed source to debunk some of the trailer trash thinking. $5–$10

Flash Facts on MOBILE HOMES

MOBILE HOME FAMILIES*

MOBILE HOMES MANUFACTURERS ASSOCIATION

"Flash Facts On Mobile Homes"

Informational advertising brochure, four-fold, 3.5" x 7.25" folded, 17" x 7.25" unfolded, 10 page panels, by Mobile Homes Manufacturers Association, dated June 1969. The document defined a mobile home as "a portable unit designed and built to be towed on its own chassis, comprised of frame and wheels, connected to utilities, and designed without a permanent foundation for year-round living." Notice that length was not part of the definition. Interestingly, however, in discussing design features, this brochure referred to the average lengths of mobile homes measuring between 29' to 65'—a substantial variance! $10–$15

Marquis: "The Stars of I Love Lucy . . . Lucille Ball . . . Desi Arnaz . . . The Long, Long Trailer . . . The Towne . . . Milwaukee Movie Theatre."

Unused tourist postcard, black-and-white photo from the book *Images of America* by Arcadia Publishing, unnumbered, 5.75" x 4.25", copyright 2010. Marvelous find! Here is a photo of the touring tow car and lengthy trailer that promoted the wildly popular 1954 movie, which car and house trailer just happened to be setting in front of a movie theatre showing the film. A lot of moviegoers were impressed by the apparent fact that Lucy and Desi liked the big trailer house, and, in turn, the movie was used to promote mobile-home sales. (See the next picture.) $10–$15

"See New Moon Mobile Apartment Homes . . . The Long, Long Trailer, starring Lucille Ball and Desi Arnaz . . . Learn how you too can enjoy Carefree Living . . . at a new, low cost."

Magazine advertisement, in *National Geographic*, 6.75" x 10", 1954. Here, Lucy and Desi were pictured in front of a New Moon coach. $10–$15

"Vagabond" (Showing a hobo with a knapsack over his shoulder)

Metal house trailer and travel trailer emblem, 6" x 3", c. 1940s–1950s. This emblem had been affixed to a vintage trailer house. Although Vagabond was a highly successful, quality coach, it undoubtedly did not help the image of trailer houses and mobile homes to be associated with vagabonds and hobos. $30-$40

An international sensation! Caption (in Spanish language) "Despues De La Boda . . . Lucille Ball–Desi Arnaz."

Theatre lobby advertising card, cardboard, 16.25" x 12.5", c. 1954. This successful movie was shown in numerous other countries, and the mobile home became an international success, too. $20–$25

"The New Imperial '4100' . . . in the regal manner."

Advertising bi-fold brochure by Imperial Mobile Homes Company, four pages, 11" x 8.5" folded (22" x 8.5" unfolded), c. 1960s. Notice that the metal emblem in the adjacent picture is shown in the lower left-hand corner of this handsome brochure. This ad campaign, emphasizing the high-end "regal" nature of the company's mobile homes, is the type of promotion designed to debunk the less favorable view of the mobile home. $15–$20

"Imperial . . . State Line, Pennsylvania" (Showing a majestic ancient armored helmet and fleur-de-lis symbols)

Metal mobile-home emblem, 3.5" x 5", c. 1960s–1970s. The name and design of this impressive emblem suggested the image the mobile home industry should have been consistently advancing. $30-$40

"Welcome to the RV/MH (Recreational Vehicle/Mobile Home) Hall of Fame . . . Museum and Library . . . Elkhart, Indiana."

Informational brochure, bi-fold, four page panels, 3.25" x 8.5" folded (6.5" x 8.5" unfolded), c. 2010s. This brochure pictures the "new" museum, which was constructed just down the highway from its former location several years ago. This facility is a wonderful resource for anyone interested in the historic social and technological developments that have led to today's recreational vehicles and mobile homes. $5–$10

Redneck Extreme Mobile Home Makeover

Soft-cover book (with 3-D pink flamingo applique) by Jeff Foxworthy, 8" x 9", 160 pages, copyright 2005. Yahoo! This creative and funny book might as well have been called *Trailer Trash Makeover*. For instance, Foxworthy says, "You might be a redneck if . . . Your security system is the latch on your screen door . . . A tree falls through your roof and you decide to leave it . . . There are more than six vehicles under tarps in your yard . . . You wonder how service stations keep their restrooms so clean . . . Directions to your house include 'turn off the paved road' . . . Your car and your house are both up on blocks . . . " Put this book on your reading list! $20–$25

"Trailer Trashed: My Dubious Efforts Toward Upward Mobility."

Hilarious! Hard-cover story book by Hollis Gillespie (whose father was a trailer salesman and who writes from a trailer in her back yard), 6" x 9.25", 266 pages, copyright 2008. Another addition for your reading list. $20–$25

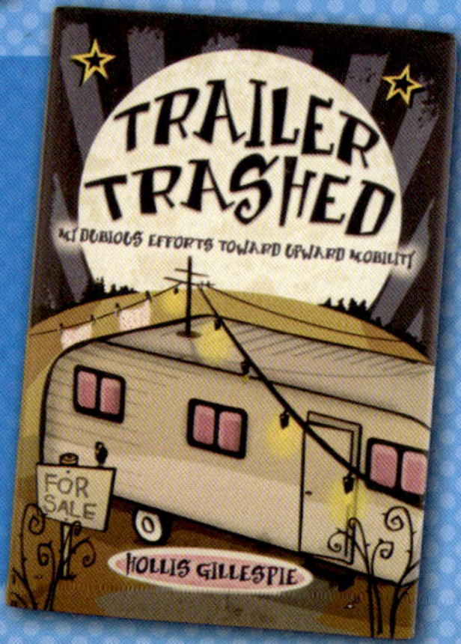

The way life should be!

"There's No Place Like Home." T-shirt logo design advertisement, cardboard black-and-white graphic, 11" x 8.5", c. 2000s. The T-shirt made with this picture on it depicted a 1940s–1950s upscale trailer house. $10–$15

People living differently than the normal inhabitants of fixed-place houses were ridiculed and derided. They were trailer trash. They seemed to have less and to live lesser lives in the eyes of the critics. These modern nomads resembled vagabonds or hobos, who were unable to live the right way in ordinary houses in established communities. But despite the criticism, trailerites persisted. The popularity of trailer houses caused an explosion in mobile-home manufacturing and in construction of mobile-home parks.

The trailer trash label has lasted for a lot of reasons. It's short and catchy. People like alliteration and brevity—so that they do not have to expend the energy to think more deeply about a subject. Those in the majority often will tolerate minority conduct, without fully approving it. And besides, there is a cottage industry of people who promote the trailer trash stereotype for fun and profit—who sell trailer trash cartoons, tee-shirts, decals, videos, postcards, books, music CDs, refrigerator magnets, and other such trinkets.

We want to caution readers about the definition of what a mobile home is. There is no precise definition, and to the extent there is a definition at all, it has undoubtedly changed somewhat over the years. A "mobile home" seems to be a self-contained house on wheels, that is nevertheless more-or-less permanently fixed in place. There is no minimum length demarcation for a coach to qualify as a mobile home. People sometimes live for long terms in very small trailers that are permanently situated

Twister Ridge Trailer Park Paper Dolls
Paper dolls book by Laura Lampe, 8.5" x 11", 16 pages folded (24.25" x 11" unfolded), copyright 1997. Scarce book! Fantastic graphic humor! The front cover is a bi-fold design of three panels, with the outside of the trailer house depicted on one side and the inside cut-a-way view of the trailer on the reverse side. Of course, also showing the female and male paper dolls. $20–$25

in one place. On the other hand, some very long coaches are towed down the highways from place to place with some frequency. See if you agree with the choices about what constitutes a mobile home in the various time periods and settings illustrated in this book.

The book's 144 pages are jam-packed with trailer trash and mobile-home memorabilia. There are nearly 400 pictures illustrating about 450 items of many kinds: decals, vintage photographs, emblems, matchbook covers, advertisements, informational brochures, magazines, playing cards, toys, and much more. Of the pieces included, 300 are postcard images. And, every piece displayed here belongs to us, from our extensive memorabilia collection.

Incidentally, every image in the book will be followed by a descriptive caption setting out what we know about the pieces, including each item's maker, composition, size, age, other details, and its estimated value. Hence, this book will also serve as a price guide for serious collectors and dealers in such memorabilia. But, a disclaimer is in order. We caution that, although we have done our very best to provide thorough and accurate information and sound valuations, some of the items are quite old and not much will be known about some of them. Further, when it comes to estimating values, reasonable minds may differ, especially when matters of taste, artistry, and fancy are involved—as is the case with many of these pieces.

Chapter 1

Before the Beginning

Which one came first—the house trailer, or the mobile home? The answer: neither one. It's a trick question; they are one-and-the-same (although the "house trailer" phrase was used before the words "mobile home"), and the process of their development took hundreds of years. Importantly, it was that long road to home mobility, which involved so many steps along the way—steps that provided humorists with chances to practice their craft before they got to the stage for their focus upon trailer trash. As examples, long ago, comedians poked fun at gypsies and gypsy wagons, at circus performers and their circus caravans, and later at tourists and their primitive travel trailers.

After the many and varied stages in the historic process that culminated in the creation of the modern mobile home, that development should have been expected. It quite naturally had to happen. People were spending extended periods in their wagons, caravans, and trailers. They were living, at least temporarily, in them. When finally the technology arrived to permit full kitchens and bathrooms to be placed in trailers, that outcome assured the explosion in mobile home popularity—especially since at about the same time, shortly after the end of World War II, there were serious housing shortages. Now, millions and millions of people live in mobile homes in many countries around the world.

Remarkable find! Reflects an earlier, and less enlightened, era of understanding of the place of native Americans

"First American Mobile Home." Advertising sheet, by Pontiac Motor Division of General Motors Corporation, unnumbered, 16.25" x 11", copyright 1955. The text described the design of the teepee, especially its mobility and portability. And, the piece concluded with this statement: "America's first 'tourists' had a truly mobile home." $15–$20

"Homestead Mobile Home Sales . . . A Sign of Progress"

Magazine advertisement, in *LIFE*, 10.25" x 13.25", dated 1969. The covered wagon of the Western frontier era has become a well-recognized symbol of one of the important forerunners of modern travel trailers and mobile homes, and it has been adopted by several companies in the camper manufacturing, campground, mobile-home construction, and mobile-home park industries. $5–$10

"Early Day Mobile Homes"

Used tourist postcard from the painting *Yoking Up In Corral* by artist W. H. Jackson, painted between 1866–1890, housed at the Nebraska State Historical Society, by Dunlap Postcard and Dexter Press, #14316-B, 5.5" x 3.5", posted 1973 from Lincoln, Nebraska, to Sarasota, Florida. Early wagons in Europe, America, and elsewhere actually served as mobile homes, for they were wheeled boxes in which, and out of which, people lived for extended periods of time. $5–$10

A Future Design in the Making?

Notice the standard house-sized door at the front of this very early wagon, suggesting where design development would go in the future—incorporating many standard house features into movable homes. (Reverse side) "Montana Sheepwagon. Sheepherder's Mobile Home." Unused tourist postcard, black-and-white photo by Mountain Magic, #PC-C-II, 6" x 4", copyright 1984. $5–$10

Advertising for Fun and Life

(Above) (On reverse side) "Covered Wagon Diorama, Ghost Town, Knott's Berry Place, Buena Park, California." Unused advertising postcard, by Paul Klieben, unnumbered, 5.5" x 3.5", copyright 1946. $5–$10

A Conestoga Wagon. "Greetings From The 'Pennsylvania Dutch Country.'"

(Below) (On reverse side) Unused tourist postcard, color photo, by Jim Hess and Dexter Press, #48787-B, 5.5" x 3.5", dated 1961. According to the text on the card, this type of wagon originated before 1720 in Lancaster County, Pennsylvania, and served the nation's needs for at least the next 130 years. These early vehicles provided people with a covered, mobile place to sleep, eat, and store their belongings for extended periods of time—like a house. $5–$10

"Caravanning In Ireland . . . What did we chat about with the folk along the road? Themselves, the weather, local yarns, the price of oats."

Fascinating vintage find! Magazine article, black-and-white graphic, from *HOLIDAY* magazine, 10.5" x 13.75", pages 91–98, April 1948. Today, travelers in campers and mobile homes do similar things—except that now we talk about the price of gasoline, instead of the price of oats that were fed to the working animals that pulled the early caravans. For the article, $10–$15

"Gypsy Camp At Sundown."

Scarce game. Jigsaw puzzle in original box, over 400 pieces, by Good Companion, #52, puzzle 19.5" x 13.5", box 10" x 7.5" x 1.5", c. 1960s. This old puzzle made the connection between gypsies, gypsy wagons, and camping, lest children might forget it. And, the trailer trash stereotype lingered close by in the background. $10–$15

"Fox Hunting."

(On reverse side) Here, the upscale fox hunt was depicted racing past the poor gypsies and their small wagon parked (with a cooking fire underway) in the background. This scene was symbolic of the real-world process and was part of the confirmation process of the stereotype about trailer-house living. Used British tourist postcard, oilette, by Tuck and Sons, #9450, 5.5" x 3.5", posted 1909 from Normanton to Leeds, England. $10–$15.

"Our Caravan. The Simple Life."

(On reverse side) Unused British tourist postcard, photo oilette, by Tuck and Sons, #511, 3.5" x 5.5", c. 1900s. The implicit message associated with the "simple" life of gypsies and their wagon undoubtedly suggested a nomadic, impoverished, and difficult life—trailer trash. $10–$15

"Gypsy . . . KOT1633."

Used (but not posted) QSL postcard, by QSL Publishing, 5.5" x 3.5", c. 1970s. Fun QSL postcard that shows an amateur radio antenna on the roof of the gypsy wagon. The graphics on this card suggest that the radio operators who created the card probably had some kind of mobile home or trailer that allowed them to travel around with their radio equipment. $5–$10

Wonderfully detailed circus caravan "toy"-not really intended for play by children. (On box sides) "Dodgem Truck and Caravan . . . Fairground Attractions."

Die-cast scale model toy and original box, 1:50 scale, circus performers' residential caravan, by Corgi (Great Britain), #CC11506, box 16.5" x 5.25" x 2.5", dated 2002. The old circus performers' caravans resembled gypsy wagons and trolley cars (with the trolley-style roof designs). Circus performers had to have a place to live while on the nomadic circus routes; these caravans satisfied that need, and the circus caravans served as one more of the roll models for the modern mobile home. $40-$50

A day at the beach cabana/caravan for mother, daughter, and the family dog

Unused tourist postcard, no maker identified, unnumbered, 3.5" x 5.5", c. 1900s. The coach pictured on this colorful card appeared to be a beach cabana, or a beach house caravan, because it was so small and had such a narrow wheel base. These units were very compact because they were used by prim and proper Victorians only for changing before and after swimming and sunbathing. Again, such vehicles served as another type of roll model for later developments, including mobile homes. See the next two cards as well. $10–$15

"Scheveningen. Badkoetsen Gemengde Baden."

Unused international tourist postcard, color photo, by Ultgave Sjouke, #152, 5.5" x 3.5", c. 1900s. Note that some of the small beach cabanas pictured on this card, and the next one as well, have flat roofs, and some have peaked roofs—a variation still seen today among modern mobile homes. $10–$15

"Scheveningen."

Unused international tourist postcard, black and white, by Vivat, #3072, 5.5" x 3.5", c. 1900s. This photo shows two early beach caravans right next to one another at the water's edge. Can you see the swimmer standing on the beach in his striped, full-length bathing suit? $15–$20

Forerunners of the modern mobile home at work on the farm fields, serving as meal wagons and cook's quarters

Two unused tourist postcards, black-and-white photos, no maker identified, unnumbered, 5.5" x 3.5", c. 1910s–1920s. These two photos appear to show two views of the opposite ends of the same wagon, taken at different times. In one scene, you can see some of the workers' teepee-type tents in the background. These boxes on wheels started life as farm wagons, and they were used as cook houses and/or bunk houses on farms and ranches throughout the US and Canada. Such units served as important roll models for the modern mobile home because they incorporated both cooking inside the trailer and sleeping arrangements (the cooks would often sleep in the meal wagons). Notice the stovepipe protruding through the roof. See the cards that follow, too. Each, $10–$15

Two views of the same farm cook house on wheels

Two unused tourist postcards, black-and-white photos, no maker identified, unnumbered, 5.5" x 3.5", c. 1910s–1920s. The same two ladies appear in both pictures, and they must have been the cooks for the farmhands shown. Notice that this cook-house trailer incorporated both an inside stove (as confirmed by the roof-top stovepipe) and an awning that served to cool the coach and to allow food to be handed through the opening to the hungry farmhands. Each, $10–$15

(In French) "Contre la crise du Logement . . . La Roulotte Des Jeunes Epoux."

Unused tourist postcard, by Kiss (printed in France), #862, 5.5" x 3.5", c. 1910s. The antique caravan depicted here was a clean, neat, upscale wagon (with shutters and two stovepipes) and with a well-dressed and amorous couple inside. We like the dog and cat, too. $10–$15

Bull power at work! "J.S. Myers. Premont, Tex to New York City."

Unused tourist postcard, black-and-white photo, no maker identified, unnumbered, 5.5" x 3.5", c. 1920s. We wonder how long it would take two big bulls to drag that old house wagon all the way from Texas to New York City, and we wonder whether they made it. $10–$15

Two more agriculture-based role models for the modern mobile home

Two unused tourist postcards, black-and-white photos, no maker identified, unnumbered, 5.5" x 3.5", c. 1910s–1920s. The house trailer could not be far away. Each, $15–$20

More weekenders?

Unused tourist postcard, black-and-white photo, no maker identified (either US or British), unnumbered, 3.5" x 5.5", c. 1910s–1920s. The dapper fellows posing here seemed quite proud of their caravan. Notice the split door style. $15–$20

Weekend gypsies? City slickers at play with their caravans in the country

Remarkably, the early cards on this page seem to show small caravans being enjoyed for purely recreational use. Two tourist postcards (one used with a partially illegible postmark, one unused), black-and-white photos, one by Paget Prize with a British stamp, the other by VEF, unnumbered, 5.5" x 3.5" (one with scalloped edges), one posted in 1905, one c. 1900s–1910s. Notice that the one caravan, named "The Rambler," sported a trolley-style raised roof down the center of the coach where headroom was needed. Each, $15–$20

Scarce card! Caption: "British-Israel Caravan Mission."

Used missionary informational postcard, black-and-white photo, by R. Banks (London), unnumbered, 5.5" x 3.5", posted 1904 from/to New South wales (postmark/address partially illegible). Notice the price per dozen for the cards, which would have been used to announce itineraries and meetings and to spread the mission's message. Note also the raised trolley roof design to allow for headroom down the center of the coach where people would walk and stand. See the below card as well. $20–$25

Yet another roll model for the modern mobile home

"Ready for the Road, Cecil Barrie's Empire Palace Car. Touring England, Ireland, Scotland and Wales." Used tourist postcard, black-and-white photo, by Senior and Co., unnumbered, 5.5" x 3.5", posted 1908 from Exton to Clipsham, England. Notice the curtains in the windows and the raised trolley roof section of this early British horse-drawn caravan. We like the Terrier dog that seemed fascinated by the large horses. $15–$20

(In French) "Salon de 1905. La Roulotte du Pere Andre, par Amell-Jorda."

Unused tourist postcard, black-and-white photo, by SPA, #729, 5.5" x 3.5" dated 1905. This scene of so much stuff scattered outside on the ground beside the little caravan, with the dog standing guard, suggested that the elderly occupants were peasants. Early trailer trashing. $15–$20

(In German) "Wir ziehen und schieben mit starker Hand dieses Haus: 'Rund um Deuschland!'"

Unused tourist postcard, black-and-white photo, printed in Germany, 5.5" x 3.5", dated 1931. $10–$15

Two British church/missionary caravans

Unused missionary informational postcards, black-and-white photos, no makers identified, one unnumbered, one #539, 5.5" x 3.5", c. 1900s. Each, $10–$15

Rare card! "Trailing Along!"

It was LONG all right! Unused comic postcard, black and white, by Val-Stef, #A17, 3.5" x 5.5", copyright 1952. This very clever card predated by only a couple of years the classic movie *The Long, Long Trailer* of 1954. Some trailer coaches were growing in length to more readily satisfy customers who were going to live full-time in them as mobile homes. $25–$30

COMMANDER GATTI
Returns from BELGIAN CONGO
with Great Enthusiasm for
INTERNATIONAL TRUCKS

THE EQUATORIAL HEART OF DARKEST AFRICA

Commander and Mrs. Gatti,—from the frontispiece of their book, "Great Mother Forest," published by Charles Scribner's Sons.

The de luxe caravan in the village of Niangara. All the trucks are standard chassis, as sold by your dealer.

COMMANDER ATTILIO GATTI, famed African explorer who two years ago set out for the equatorial jungle with his luxurious "Jungle Yacht" expedition, has returned to America with all his objectives accomplished. He returns, moreover, from his tenth Congo venture with a world of praise for his five International Trucks.

Commander Gatti writes International Harvester: "I do not know what importance you attribute to my testimony, but I assure you I do not give it lightly. I could not exaggerate my great admiration for this so perfect performance! The work of these trucks is what I had dreamed of so many years in Africa.

"In my nine earlier expeditions I had tried so many trucks and suffered with so many. My first travels were by camel in 1919. I then used Italian trucks, then French, then English. My sixth *safari* was powered by well-known American trucks. Always there was chronic grief and trouble . . . But finally at Nairobi my eyes were opened when I first used an International, and it was a *second-hand* truck. That battered old vehicle had already lived through years of terrible African punishment when I bought it for a song and put a native driver on it. But what I then saw from day to day was truly a revelation.

"That is why the 'Jungle Yacht' expedition *had to be* International-powered. I congratulate myself, and I congratulate your company on a magnificent product!"

• • •

Write for the free booklet covering Commander Gatti's long career on the Dark Continent. It contains 74 illustrations and is packed with information about the mysterious African interior. Return the coupon or simply send a penny post card.

INTERNATIONAL HARVESTER COMPANY
182 North Michigan Ave. Chicago, Illinois

The beautiful living room and observation-dining car, with library, desk, and bar. Note indirect lighting, telephone, and two-way radio. There are also two perfectly appointed bedrooms and an all-electric kitchen. Each stainless-steel trailer unit is 40 feet in length.

• • •

"These crude African dirt roads are flooded by the rainy seasons and amputated in long stretches by maddened streams; thrown up and down crazy mountain chains in unbelievable hairpin turns and climbs." —Commander Gatti.

A few of the 70 wives of the Mangbetu king, Ekibondo. Note the elongated skulls, resulting from binding the heads of babies, beginning two hours after they are born.

INTERNATIONAL HARVESTER COMPANY
182 North Michigan Ave. Chicago, Ill.
Please mail me, free, Commander Gatti's own fascinating story of his adventures.
Name ______
Address ______ *State* ______
City ______

INTERNATIONAL TRUCKS

Scarce piece! "Commander Gatti Returns From Belgian Congo With Great Enthusiasm For International Trucks"

Magazine advertisement, color and black-and-white photos, in *Collier's* magazine, 10.5" x 13.5", page 25, June 9, 1940. These custom-made, futuristic, motorized "Jungle Yacht" coaches were used on a notable two-year expedition—and were certainly the first modern mobile homes to have arrived in Africa. $30–$40

Spectacular, rare find! "Nomad Motor Caravan"

Unused advertising postcard, black-and-white photo, no maker identified, unnumbered, long 9.5" x 4", c. 1930s. A novel idea! Here, two long trailers could be married together at the rear of each, by backing them together—with a curtained platform providing a passageway between them. What a roomy mobile home this would have made! $40–$50

Lavish idea! Railroad cars as mobile home roll models! "L.N.E.R. Camping Coach"

Unused British advertising postcard, black-and-white photo, no maker identified, unnumbered, 5.5" x 3.5", c. 1940s. The printed text on the card's reverse side touted that these camping coaches "accommodate six persons and are equipped with every requisite for a camping holiday" (and they rented for 300 pounds a week). This railroad coach was basically a temporary mobile home on rails. $10–$15

Another railway mobile vacation home. "An LMS Holiday Caravan."

Unused British advertising postcard, black-and-white photo, no maker identified, unnumbered, 5.5" x 3.5", c. 1940s. $10–$15

Chapter 2

A New Tradition

From the earliest beginnings of the travel-trailer craze, those small dwellings on wheels were often called house trailers, trailer houses, and mobile homes. With their creation, there needed to be places to park them. Mobile-home parks were developed, and they grew and grew. Comics had a field day making fun of them. After all, humorists had already accumulated a large inventory of barbs to fire at the trailer trash in mobile-home parks, as the result of the many similar issues they had targeted at early campgrounds. The possibilities seemed endless: there were crowded conditions, pet and wildlife mishaps, outhouse issues, hillbilly and flirtatious neighbors, noise problems, swimming pool and shuffleboard encounters, weather emergencies, and on and on. No wonder all mobile home owners seemed vulnerable to the trailer trash charge.

Yet, what really happened was that thousands of clean, modern, comfortable mobile-home parks occupied by decent, hardworking, courteous people opened and flourished. The financial backing was there to support the new parks. The dramatic explosion of good, and even upscale, mobile-home parks resulted from operation of the economic laws of supply and demand. A new lifestyle tradition evolved. And, this *new* tradition has stood the test of time, for it has already lasted for nearly a century.

Remarkable find! Antique British trailer trash humor! "The Caravan Craze Scene in a lonely part of the Highlands"

Newspaper cartoon, black-and-white graphic, in *Punch*, or the *London Charivari*, 6" x 4.5", July 19, 1911, page 66. Outstanding drawing of horse-drawn caravans of the era. We are not certain whether the main thrust of the comedy was aimed at the trailers, or the Scotts (or maybe both). $15–$20

Symbolizing the new tradition of mobile home living. "Homecrest Mobile Home Park . . . E 458"

Fabric triangular patch, no maker identified, 7" x 5.5" x 5.5", c. 1950s–1960s. Unusual find! This type of emblem would have been suitable for affixing to a sweater or jacket. Since the text appears to identify the lot site in the park (E 458), perhaps this patch was a symbol for a block club or group within the trailer park. $10–$15

Early English caravans

Two early, unused postcards, black-and-white photos, 5.5" x 3.5", c. 1920s–1930s. The upper card showing a rather primitive site was captioned: "The Camping Ground, Morfa Bychan," #MFAB.21, by Frith Ltd. The lower card, which appears to illustrate a very early caravan permanently located as a house, bears an old handwritten note dated June 6, 1923. Each, $10–$15

Two vintage photos of proud owners posing outside their trailer houses

Black-and-white snapshots, no makers or numbers identified, one 5" x 3.5", the other 3.5" square, both with scalloped edges, one dated 1954, the other c. 1950s. Each, $5–$10

Fun, group-picture, panorama postcard! "Lowe's City Cottage and Trailer Park" (St. Petersburg, Florida)

Unused advertising postcard, color photo, by Schatzman Advertising, #42,230F, 9" x 3.5", c. 1950s. This scene must have attracted just about all of the residents of this trailer park, having 200 sites. Reading the text on the back of these vintage cards sometimes creates nostalgic bliss—for instance, as this card's text referred to the availability of square and round dancing, bingo, and two telephones! $15–$20

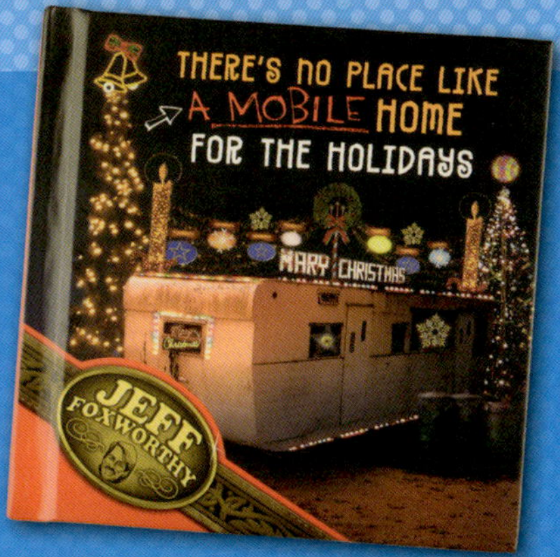

Wonderful graphic! "Joe's Trailer Home . . . Why, everything's changed overnight!"

And, not for the better! Magazine cartoon, black-and-white graphic, *New Yorker*, 8" x 11.5", c. 1940s. This fun cartoon focused on the explosion of family size (note all the little children) and of the popularity in travel trailers and house trailers after World War II (note the crowded trailer park). Plus, other trailer trash elements were depicted as well, such as the outdoor food preparation, the stray dogs, and the used tire being rolled down the road. $10–$15.

There's No Place Like A Mobile Home For The Holidays

Humorous little hardcover book by comedian Jeff Foxworthy, 6.25" square, 66 pages (with included CD Redneck *12 Days of Christmas*), copyright 2004. In Foxworthy's memorable "T'was the Night after Christmas," he begins by setting the peaceful scene at the mobile home: "T'was the night after Christmas and all through the trailer, The beer had gone flat and the pizza was staler" (page 48). He persuasively and frequently, with enthusiasm, promotes the trailer trash theme. We love his comedy. $10–$15

Oh . . . the good life in a mobile home.

Two unused tourist postcards, black-and-white photos, no maker identified, unnumbered, 5.5" x 3.5", c. 1950s. Each, $5–$10

"Yellow Rose of Texas . . . Tyler State Park . . . Tyler, Texas"

(Reverse side) Unused art postcard, reproduction from a painting by artist Paige Bridges, unnumbered, large 8.5" x 5.5", c. 2000s. We love the works of our friend Paige Bridges, whose specialty is RV art like the spectacular scene displayed here and throughout this book. Find her pieces at VintageTravelTrailerArt.com. $10–$15

"Sarasota Mobile Home Park" (Sarasota, Florida)

Used advertising postcard, by E. N. Hamilton, #16214, 5.5" x 3.5", posted 1957 from Sarasota, Florida, to Kalamazoo, Michigan. $10–$15

"Trailerama"

Spectacular and fun publication! Hardbound coffee-table style book by Phil Noyes, published by Gibbs Smith, 11" x 9", 192 pages, copyright 2012. When you pick up this book and start to examine it, be prepared not to be able to put it down for a couple of hours. And, you won't want it to come to an end. It's about the colorful memorabilia and history of the travel trailer (and the house trailer, since there was really no line of demarcation between those objects in their formative years—see his cover graphic). $25–$30.

"Spring Thaw"

(On reverse side) Unused art postcard, reproduction from a painting by Paige Bridges, unnumbered, 5.5" x 4.25", copyright 2009. The vintage mobile home shown here appears to be a Spartan, a popular quality brand also illustrated later in this chapter. $5–$10

From 1937! "Trailer Trails . . . A New Game of Skill and Chance . . . A Trailer Full of Fun for Adults and Children."

Board game box, 14.5" x 9" x 1.25", by Offset-Gravure Corp. and Gazley-Harrington, copyright 1937. One of the earliest games featuring travel trailers and house trailers. With marvelous vintage color graphics. $40–$50

A personal favorite of ours! "God Bless Our Trailer Home"

Metal kitchen trivet, no maker identified, unnumbered, 4.25" x 4.75", c. 1950s–1960s. Stunning bright yellow coach graphic! See the next piece as well. $15–$20

More "Trailer Trails"

Here is the game board for Trailer Trails, which measures 17.25" x 13.5" and also features handsome graphics—showing trailer camps and trailers throughout Canada, Mexico, and the USA. Although the idea of this fun 1937 game was to move the trailers around the map, we know the reality was that World War II came along and disrupted real life. After the war, many trailers did not move much because they became housing for returning GIs and their young families. Next, many of the trailers got larger and were permanently sited to serve as permanent housing for even larger families. Thus, the mobile home tradition began. Note the many not-so-subtle trailer trash suggestions on this game board—such as "Wait one turn to chase animal (a skunk) from kitchen," "Draw bar breaks on trailer—Go to Chicago for repair," "Stop one turn to stock the pantry with tamales" (near Mexico City), "Indian stowaway in the shower bath—Go back 6 spaces," and "Mother puts the laundry out to dry—Wait one turn."

"Trailer Court . . . Tustin, Wis."

(Above) Unused advertising postcard, black-and-white photo, no maker identified, #5, 5.5" x 3.5", c. 1940s. Of course, in the early era of mobile homes, they were most popular in the warm-weather states, rather than in the northern tier of winter-weather states. As insulation and heating for coaches improved, more and more mobile homes found resting places up north. $5–$10

"Dodson's Park Avenue Trailer Court . . . Sanford, Fla."

(Below) Unused advertising postcard, black-and-white photo, by Raymond Studio and Dexter Press, unnumbered, 5.5" x 3.5", c. 1940s–1950s. The early mobile homes pictured here were set up with permanent screen rooms or patios attached to the coaches, which added a lot of additional enclosed living space. $5–$10

A family portrait

(Above) Black-and-white photo, no maker identified, unnumbered, 4" x 4.5", c. 1940s. As with one of the adjacent pictures, here is another soldier standing in front of an early mobile home in a mobile-home park—presumably posed with his family members, including the dog. Of course, to deal with the existing post-World War II housing shortage, both mobile homes and mobile-home parks were needed. $5–$10

Two sisters, or twins?

(Below) Black-and-white photo, no maker identified, unnumbered, 4.5" x 3.25", c. 1940s. The lovely ladies pictured here were standing in front of a lengthy and impressive early mobile home (although the makeshift cinder-block entry step was not so impressive). $5–$10

"You may not find a house in every place you roam . . . But when you own a Spartan you always have a Home . . . Spartan Aircraft Company . . . Tulsa, Oklahoma."

Magazine advertisement, color graphics, in *National Geographic*, 6.75" x 10", dated 1953. This creative ad, by a company that started out in aircraft manufacturing, spoke of Spartan Mobile Homes being "Modern as Tomorrow" and possessing "lifetime exteriors" (which, like Airstream trailers, were designed with aluminum, like aircraft fuselages). $5–$10

Isn't it lovely? "God Bless This Mobile Home."

Decorative ceramic plate, by Norcrest, made in Japan, unnumbered, 7.5" round, c. 1960s. Part of the process of establishing a tradition is the creation of memorabilia to commemorate it, in this instance mobile home living. $10–$15

Attention! "A61"

(Above) Black-and-white photo, no maker identified, unnumbered, 4" x 3.5", c. 1940s. With the housing shortage for soldiers returning from World War II, they and their families needed places to live—and mobile homes fit the bill. This soldier wearing his uniform stood inside the picket-fenced lot for his mobile home (bearing #A.61), and other similarly fenced coaches stood in neat rows established with military precision. $5–$10

"#A.61" (again).

(Below) Black-and-white photo, no maker identified, unnumbered, 4" x 3.5", c. 1940s. These two pictures show the same mobile home. $5–$10

"Venetian Trailer Park . . . St. Petersburg, Fla."

(Above) Unused advertising postcard, black-and-white photo, by National Press, unnumbered, 5.5" x 3.5", c. 1950s. Note the prominent window and patio awnings, the landscape plantings, and picket-fence skirting under the perimeter of the home—all suggesting that this mobile home was staying put for a long time. $5–$10

Vintage British Caravan.

(Below) Black-and-white photo, no maker identified, unnumbered, 5.25" x 3.25", c. 1930s–1940s. Of course, the negative impact of the long years of World War II on English coach building slowed the whole process of development and improvement of mobile homes and their parks. Notice the covering of the tires (to protect them from the deteriorating effects of extended sun exposure). $5–$10

Handsome 1940s-1950s house trailer

(Above) Used tourist postcard, black-and-white photo, no maker identified, unnumbered, 5.5" x 3.5", posted 1952 from Hines, Minnesota, to Kansas City, Missouri. The sender was actually visiting at this location and called it the "Black Duck Resort" in Hines. The large coach in this picture sported two round portal-style windows in the side entry doors. $10–$15

How'd they do that?

(Below) Black-and-white photo, no markings, 5.75" x 3.5", c. 1950s. Notice that this impressive looking house trailer has its tongue/hitch elevated and resting on concrete blocks on a hillside, which means that it was somehow towed forward into its resting position. One reason would be to have the side entry door(s) on the up-slope of the terrain, rather than opening to a drop-off. $5–$10

"Mobilehome And Trailer Parks In New Hampshire"

Informational tri-fold brochure, black and white, by New Hampshire Division of Economic Development, 4" x 9", six page segments, dated 1964. Good idea! This basic directory identified some forty parks in the state and certainly would have fostered a variety of business activities. The cover graphic showed four mobile homes at rest in New Hampshire. Most importantly, the brochure also served as an official welcome and approval by the state about the presence of mobile homes and their residential parks. $5–$10

Fantastic resource! Trailer Coach Homes

Advertising paperback book, color cover photos, by Fawcett Books, #163, 6.5" x 9.5", 144 pages, copyright 1952. This detailed photographic and textual presentation of both the exterior and interior components of mobile homes by forty coach brands ranged from ABC and All-States, to Whitley and Zimmer models. $30-$40

"Rekreatieoord Distelloo . . . Helvoirt."

(Above) (On reverse side) Unused tourist postcard, black-and-white photo, no maker identified, #1068, 5.5" x 3.5", c. 1960s–1970s. A simple, attractive Scandinavian house trailer or caravan. $5–$10

"Saundersfoot Bay Caravan Park, Suandersfoot, Pembs" (England)

(Below) Unused advertising postcard, black-and-white photo, no maker identified, unnumbered, 5.75" x 4", c. 1960s. What wonderful, scenic hillside home sites for these trailer houses, complete with distant water views. $5–$10

"Weiner's Trailer Sales and Service . . . Between Leighton and Parryville, Penna."

(Above) Unused advertising postcard, black-and-white photo, by J .C. Mankos and Dexter Press, #12320-B, 5.5" x 3.5", c. 1950s–1960s. At the early stage of mobile home development, large mobiles (like several in this picture) were still being called simply "trailers" in many places. And, that shorthand label was not helpful. $5–$10

This vintage picture might be captioned "A Family Affair."

(Below) Mobile homes were, after all, homes in which the family would live, and this lifestyle would become a new tradition for millions of people around the globe. Black-and-white photo, no markings, 3.5" square, c. 1950s. This photo showed eight people—adults and children—posing in front of a classic mobile home. $5–$10

"Trail-R-News . . . The Complete Mobile Home Magazine . . . The Only American Magazine Where Editors Live And Travel In Trailers."

Magazine cover and full issue, black-and-white cover photo, 8" x 11", 102 pages, March 1958. Can a true tradition be established without at least one magazine devoted to the subject? We don't think so. For the issue, $10–$15

"Trailer Living At Its Best In Beautiful Star Trailer Park . . . Tacoma, Washington."

(Above) (On Reverse side) Used advertising postcard, color photo, by Mike Roberts and Color Card, #SC1911, posted 1961 from Tacoma, Washington, to Portland, Oregon. You can always tell which coaches are permanent or long-term residences by the appearances of the exterior elements—patios, screen rooms, flowers, landscaping, and such. The house trailers shown here appear to be fixed in place for the duration. $5–$10

Handsome portal windows adorn both side entry doors of this long trailer house.

(Below) Black-and-white photo, no maker identified, unnumbered, 5.5" x 3.5", with scalloped edges, dated 1953. One good rule-of-thumb is that mobile homes tend to have two side entry doors (because they ordinarily are longer), whereas travel trailers usually have only one entry door (because they commonly are shorter). $5–$10

Vintage English caravan

Black-and-white photo, no maker, unnumbered, 5.5" x 3.5", c. 1940s–1950s. The handsome metal fencing pictured here seemed perfectly sized for this smaller house trailer, which according to a note on the back of the photo belonged to a lady in Enfield, Middlesex. $5–$10

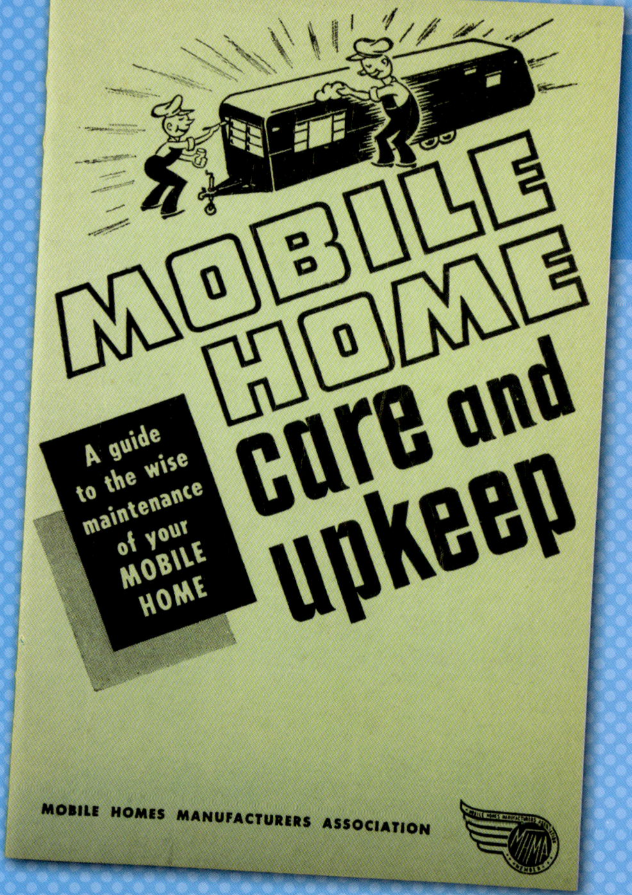

Mobile Home Care And Upkeep . . . A Guide To The Wise Maintenance Of Your Mobile Home

Complimentary informational booklet, by Mobile Homes Manufacturers Association, 5.5" x 8.5", 34 pages, copyright 1955. For the booklet, $10–$15

"Home Sweet Home, On Wheels"

Black-and-white photos, no makers identified, unnumbered, 3.5" square, with scalloped edges, one dated 1956, one c. 1950s. Just about every attempt was made to treat trailer homes like ordinary houses, such as the provision of landscaping and the installation of fencing (a white picket fence) in one of those pictures. Each, $5–$10

"Plaza Mobile Court . . . Bradenton, Fla."

Used advertising postcard, black-and-white photo, by L. L. Cook Co., #12-M, 5.5" x 3.5", posted 1961 from Bradenton, Florida, to Traverse City, Michigan. The senders wrote, in their message on the back of this card featuring a well-appointed mobile home and side yard, that: "It's beautiful here. You would love the flowers." $5–$10

Chapter 3

Let's Make a Deal

What would we do without mobile homes as the brunt of so many jokes and insults? Oh . . . the images of run-down, dilapidated, and unoccupied trailers situated in tiny yards adorned and even overflowing with worn-out appliances, empty beer bottles and aluminum cans, and derelict pick-up trucks and their spare tires—always with "for rent" or "for sale" signs. Who ever makes one of those deals? Who would ever think of buying a brand new mobile home?

The real story, on the other hand, paints a very different picture. The mobile home industry has become big business, really big business, in spite of constant trailer trash bashing. There are so many sizes, floor-plans, and colors of new and good used coaches. Of course, the expansive advertising campaigns have fostered consumer interest and even excitement about the advantages of mobile home living—such as the convenience and savings to be realized by buying a brand new or recent, completely modern, fully furnished, and movable home. It can be a dream come true! Let's make a deal—which was the aim of many of the pieces pictured in this chapter.

"Trailer No. 13, Bombay Beach, California, 1993."
(Reverse side) Unused tourist postcard, color photo, by Jeff Brouws and Chronicle Books, unnumbered, 5.5" x 4", dated 2003. Just a little buffing and paint, and it will be as good as new? We don't think so. $5–$10 (for the card, not the trailer).

"Nobody's Home, Butler County, Pennsylvania."
(Reverse side) Unused tourist postcard, black-and-white photo, by James Soffer and Last Shot Inc., unnumbered, 6" x 4", dated 1994. The wind must have blown the "For Rent" sign away. $5–$10

Spectacular antique view of an early "mobile home"

(Above) "Bohemians." Used tourist postcard, color photo, no maker identified, unnumbered, 5.5" x 3.5", posted 1904 from Brighton to Chichester, England. We wonder how much these early coaches would have cost? $10–$15.

"Gipsies."

(Below) Unused tourist postcard, "oilette" painting, by Tuck and Sons, #754, 5.5" x 3.5", c. 1900s. $10–$15.

"You Have No Idea What You're Missing" and "Home Is Where A Body's Happy . . ."

Unused tourist postcards, linen, by Curteich, Time Saver Comics and Trailer Comics series, #C-1187 and #C-183, 5.5" x 3.5", c. 1940s. The marvelous graphics on these cards shows a hillbilly house on wheels (named "Roll Along Home"), complete with an attached chicken coup, laundry drying on a clothesline on the roof, the pet Fido's dog house (also on wheels), and a skinny cow grazing on the front yard. Do you think this fun mobile home was homemade or factory-built? Each, $10–$15

"Tornado . . . Awning From Mobile Home Dangles From Overhead Line."

(Above) (On reverse side) Press photo, black and white, 8.5" x 5.75", dated 1969. This scene had played out in Polk County, Florida, and it does show how vulnerable mobile homes can be to severe weather. $10–$15

"Kropf Eldorado . . . Kropf Mfg. Co. Inc. . . . Goshen, Ind."

(Below) Mobile home advertising emblem, heavy metal, 8" x 2", c. 1950s–1960s. This worn and rusty emblem, which would have been affixed to the side of a newly constructed mobile home, appears as though it may have suffered through a flood or tornado, or both. $30–$40

"Part Of The Damage From Friday's Rash Of Storms"

(On reverse side) Press photo, black and white, 9" x 7", dated 1971. Amazing image showing a Florida mobile home that had been flipped upside down by Mother Nature. $10–$15

"Let Your Choice Be American For Your Mobile Living Happiness and Contentment" (Cassopous, Michigan)

Marvelous graphic! Unused advertising postcard, black-and-white photos on yellow background, no maker identified, #1255, 3.5" x 5.5", c. 1950s–1960s. Scarce card—illustrating coaches of 32' to 45' in length. $20–$25

"Airport Trailer Sales . . . Cedar Rapids, Iowa"

Unused advertising postcard, chrome, by U. O. Colson Co., #25,065F, 5.5" x 3.5", c. 1950s–1960s. Sophisticated looking coach! $10–$15

We like this caption "Holly Park Homes Make Happy People."

(on reverse side) Unused advertising postcard, color photo, by Photo-Matic Corp., #091237, 5.5" x 3.5", c. 1960s. This coach was large and inviting. $5–$10

"Pennsylvania Trailer Sales"

Unused advertising postcard, linen, by Mellinger Studios, #82992, 5.5" x 3.5", c. 1950s. The mobile home on this bright card reminds us of the impressive coach in Lucy and Desi's movie *The Long, Long Trailer*. $15–$20

"1953 Detroiter . . . Detroiter Coach Company . . . Detroit, Michigan."

Stunning picture! Magazine advertisement, 8.25" x 11.5", in *Trailer Topics Magazine*, 1953. What a sizable, fabulous, upscale mobile home. $10–$15

Handsome mobile home!

Unused advertising postcard, color photo, no maker identified, unnumbered, 5.5" x 3.5", c. 1950s. The interesting, vintage text printed on the reverse side: "The 2-bedroom Newport Pride is America's greatest mobile home value. It's completely furnished and includes bath with shower. Only $2,995 plus tax." Times, and mobile home prices, have changed dramatically! Notice the reference to the self-contained bathroom, which was a recent advancement in mobile home technology in that era. $10–$15

"Rollohome Corporation, Marshfield, Wisconsin"

Unused advertising postcard, color photo, by E. C. Kropp, #4600N, 5.5" x 3.5", c. 1950s. Notice how well the porthole windows and the baby-moon hubcaps embellish the style of this sizable mobile home. It was both simple and sophisticated. $10–$15

"Marlette Coach Company"

Used advertising postcard, chrome, no maker identified, unnumbered, 5.5" x 3.5", posted 1960 from Americus to Albany, Georgia. High-end, stylish mobile home! The text on the back of the card included this catchy rhyme: "Your Best Bet Is Still Marlette!" $10–$15

"Macoma Engineering Inc. . . . Cypress, California"

(On reverse side) Unused advertising postcard, color photo, by Aurora Postcard, #10,743A, 5.5" x 3.5", c. 1950s–1960s. The text on the rear of the card boasted: "Manufacturers of the famous 'Rod and Reel' tenwide mobile home. . . . Custom work is our specialty. Bring us your floor plan." It was a solid-looking coach. $10–$15

Fun card! "Landola"

(Above) Unused collectible postcard, reproduction of 1950s Landola trailer poster, by Country Music Foundation and Chronicle Books, 6" x 4.25", copyright 2001. $5–$10

"Landola Trailer Manufacturing Co., Swayzee, Ind., Phone 49"

(Below) Used advertising postcard, black-and-white photo, by National Press, unnumbered, 5.5" x 3.5", posted 1951 from Reynoldsburg, Ohio, to Brookston, Indiana. This upscale pair of vintage streamline coaches possesses an art-deco influence. $10–$15

"Davis Trailer Sales"

(Above) Unused advertising postcard, black-and-white aerial photo, no maker identified, unnumbered, 5.5" x 3.5", c. 1950s. The text on the back touted: "Selling the finest in Trailer Homes." Scarce card! $10–$15

"Model 41"

(Below) Used advertising postcard, black-and-white photo, by Howard Photo Service, unnumbered, 5.5" x 3.5", posted 1954 from Toledo, Ohio, to Fort Knox, Kentucky. The emblem on the upper front section of the handsome coach read "Howard" brand, and the reference to "Model 41" undoubtedly indicated that the unit was forty-one feet in length. $10–$15

MOBILE HOMES BY FAMOUS ARCHITECTS

Hardbound book by Steve Schaecher, Pomegranate Communications, 7.25" x 8.25", 64 pages, copyright 2002. We like this little book for many reasons. It is fun and thoughtful. You would enjoy seeing the extreme mobile designs. Most importantly, the book's preface declares: "And, hey, no more jokes about trailer parks and tornados …" $20–$25

"Darby Craft Coach" (Terrell, Texas)

Unused advertising postcard, color photo, by Tiny Davis and Baxtone, #C-18027, 5.5" x 3.5", c. 1950s–1960s. Outstanding picture! The company claimed, on the rear of the card, to be "Builders of Quality Homes." And, this unit really looked great! $5–$10

"I Think They've Finally Gone Too Far With The Slide-Outs."

Magazine cartoon, in *RV Journal*, 8" x 4.75", spring 2008, page 136. This very clever jab at the current popularity of slides incorporated into RVs and mobile homes goes so far as to depict slide-outs in slide-outs. $5–$10

"Condo-Minimum"

Magazine advertisement, with color photos, by American Mobile Industries, 5.5" square, in *Trailer Life*, March 1981, page 67. Clever and convincing! The text of this ad emphasized the upscale features of mobile home living, which cause it to compare favorably to condominium residency. "The luxury and livability of a fully furnished home . . . Exquisite decors. Luxurious furnishings." And, notice the slide-out section on the side of this home that expands its square footage and living area. See the slide-out features of the adjacent images as well. $5–$10

Remarkable early depiction of a slide-out, or slide-up, on this trailer house! "Camping Daze . . . Hey! Quick, do somethin'. I'm Holding Up My End!"

Unused comic tourist postcard, linen, by Curteich, Trailer Comics series, C-722, 5.5" x 3.5", c. 1940s. The slide feature in this cartoon was decades ahead of its time, especially for a two-story coach (which is not even available today). Notice also that the coach shown here had a most unusual arrangement of four wheels, one at each of its four corners. $15–$20

"Cheyenne Mobile Homes, Inc."

High-end living! Advertising card, color photo, no maker identified, unnumbered, 5.5" x 3.5", c. 1960s. Notice how much the raised area in the center of the coach's roof line helps to distinguish this unit from flat-roofed competitors. $10–$15

"Silver-Top Window Awnings"

(On reverse side) What a difference flowers can make. Unused advertising postcard, color photo, by Alpert Productions, unnumbered, 5.5" x 3.5", c. 1960s–1970s. According to the text on the back, "Silver-Top window awnings add charm and protection." $5–$10

Lovely, lovely!

Advertising card, color photo, no maker identified, unnumbered, 5.5" x 3.5", c. 1950s–1960s. The picket fence and lounge chair finish off this upscale mobile living image. $5–$10

"Triangle Trailer Sales" (El Monte, California)

Unused advertising postcard, color photo, by Lithochrome Press, unnumbered, 5.5" x 3.5", c. 1950s. Text on back: "Home of the luxurious Pan American and Paramount Trailer Coaches." $5–$10

"Sommers and Son Mobile Home Sales . . . New Port Richey, Fla."

(On reverse side) Unused advertising postcard, color photo, by Ward Beckett, #29989, 5.5" x 3.5", c. 1950s–1960s. $5–$10

"The World's Most Unusual Sign" (upside down "RIMER" sign, Greenville, South Carolina).

(On reverse side) Unused advertising postcard, color photo, by Thomas Kehoe, #S3795, 5.5" x 3.5", c. 1950s. The text explained: "A widely known landmark that particularly identifies the South's largest mobile home center . . ." $5–$10

"Reading Trailer Sales . . . Reading, Mass."

Unused advertising postcard, linen, by R. C. Shaul and E. C. Kropp, #28982N, 5.5" x 3.5", c. 1940s–1950s. The message on the back was simple: "Quality Trailers, Parts and Accessories." $10–$15

"Spectrum Of Mobile Homes, Inc." (Bradenton, Florida)

Unused advertising postcard, color photo, by Dukane Press, #R09927, 5.5" x 3.5", c. 1960s–1970s. $5–$10

"Rolland Bros. Co. Mobile Homes" (Reading, Pennsylvania)

Unused advertising postcard, color photo, by Colourpicture Publishers, #P23858, 5.5" x 3.5", 1950s–1960s. The text on the card boasted: "Penna's Largest Mobile Home Dealer." $5–$10

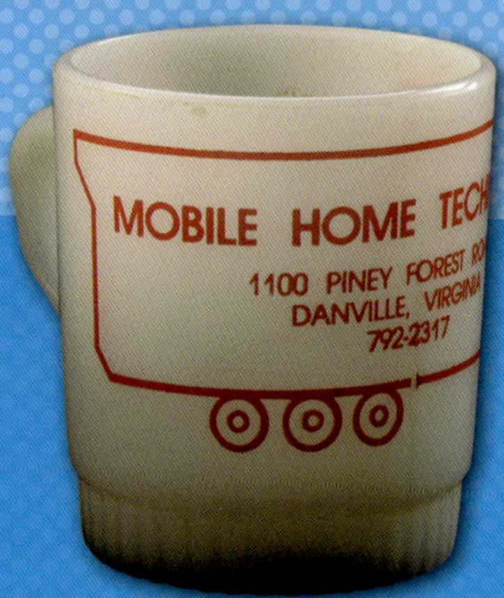

"Mobile Home Technicians . . . Danville, Virginia"

Advertising novelty, white glass drinking mug, Fire King by Anchor Hocking, 3.5" tall x 3" round, c. 1960s. $5–$10

"Schmidt Trailer Coach Co. . . . Buffalo, New York."

(On reverse side) Unused advertising postcard, color photo, by Alvin Anderson and Dexter Press, #92640, 5.5" x 3.5", c. 1950s. Size matters! $5–$10

"Model 47 Henslee 10 Wide"

(Above) Unused advertising postcard, color photo, by Walter Manning and Dexter Press, #98321, 5.5" x 3.5", c. 1950s. The text on the reverse side: "See the all new luxurious 10-wide Henslee at your local dealer." That dealer stamped its information on the card's back—"Chapman Trailer Co. . . . Houston, Texas." $5–$10

"Atlantic Trailer Corporation . . . Baltimore, Maryland"

(Below) (On reverse side) Unused advertising postcard, color photo, by Clement Erhhardt, #21119-B, 5.5" x 3.5", c. 1950s. A miniature blueprint of the coach's floor plan was printed on the back of this card, and this was a common practice. $5–$10

"Illinois Largest New Moon Dealer" and "Beal Mobile Homes . . . Olney, Illinois"

(Front/Reverse) Rare find! Advertising novelty, metal cigarette lighter, 2" x 2", c. 1950s–1960s. New Moon was a highly popular mobile home brand. $25–$30

"National Mobile Homes . . . Kalamazoo, Michigan"

(On reverse side) Unused advertising postcard, color photo, by Jay Hoops Studios, unnumbered, 6" x 3.5", c. 1950s. Often, postcards that were produced by mobile home manufacturers were distributed to local dealers, and those dealers sometimes stamped their names and contact information on the backs of the cards—as was the case here. The card was rubber-stamped by "Robbinsville Trailer Sales . . . Robbinsville, N.J." $5–$10

"Cook's Tour in a Royals"

(Above) (On reverse side) Unused advertising postcard, color photo, no maker identified, #49802-D, 5.5" x 3.5", c. 1970s–1980s. The scene was the Cook Nuclear Visitor Center near Lake Michigan, and the brand of lengthy coach shown was a Royals International from Millersburg, Indiana. As we have noted before, there is no specific length designation to separate a mobile home from a travel trailer. See the next three cards. $5–$10

"Royals Riverside Respite"

(Below) (On reverse side) Nice alliteration touch. Unused advertising postcard, color photo, no maker identified, #49803-D, 5.5" x 3.5", c. 1970s–80s. $5–$10

"Liberty Coach Company Inc. . . . Bremen, Indiana"

Grand mobile home! Advertising matchbook cover, color photo, by Matcharama Billboard and Dexter, #96020, 3" x 4.5", c. 1960s. Bright colors were popular with mobile home owners in earlier years. $5–$10

"Sold by Charleston Mobile Homes, Inc. . . . Charleston, S.C."

Handsome and rare piece! Mobile home advertising logo, metal emblem, 7.5" x 2", c. 1960s–1970s. $25–$30

"Hanson Mobile Homes . . . Kansas City, Mo." and "Kanmo Homes . . . Topeka, Kansas."

Advertising matchbook cover, color photo, by Universal Match Corp. and Dexter Press, #8171B, 3" x 4.5", c. 1950s–1960s. Notice the second-story windows on this very long mobile home. $5–$10

"Camper Country" (Myrtle Beach, South Carolina)

(Above) Unused advertising postcard, color photo, by Brandon Advertising and Dynacolor Graphics, #P30689, 5.5" x 3.5", c. 1970s–1980s. Was this *ginormous* coach a camper, or a mobile home? $5–$10

"Cavalier" (logo on the side of the coach)

(Below) Advertising card, color photo, no maker identified, unnumbered, 5.5" x 3.5", c. 1980s–1990s. $5–$10

"Drake's Mobile Homes . . . New Vienna, Ohio"

(Left) Advertising playing card, 3.5" x 2.25", c. 1960s. $5–$10

"You Get More With Crickmore Mobile Homes"

(Right) Advertising novelty, clicker metal toy, 1" x 1.75", c. 1950s–1960s. Scarce find! $15–$20

Chapter 4

Living Like a Millionaire

If you won the lottery, would you buy a mobile home? Would you live in a mobile-home park? Did you know that a lot of movie stars and celebrities have lived in mobile homes, in mobile-home parks? We know the common stereotype about permanent trailerites: they are hillbillies, who live in very old, worn-out, single-wide trailers, and whose yards resemble dump sites for rejected belongings no one else could imagine owning. But, not so fast. Those hasty impressions do not square with the realities of living in high-end mobile homes and mobile-home resorts.

Welcome to the real dream world of upscale mobile home living in this chapter. It's a life of pristine landscaping and coaches, of modern conveniences and comfort, of leisure and relaxation, of planned activities and hobbies—pure contentment and enjoyment. It's a life of some of the rich and famous. It's living like a millionaire.

Cracker Ingenuity: Tips From The Trailer Park for the Chronically Broke
Paperback book, color photo on cover, St. Martin's Griffin, by P. T. Elliott and E. M. Lowry, 5.5" x 8.25", 228 pages, copyright 2003. You know this book will be a lot of fun just by reading its title and the very first credit on its cover: "Finally, a book that shows you how to beautify your yard with old bathroom fixtures . . ." It has also been touted as the "ultimate guide to making something out of nothing." $20–$25

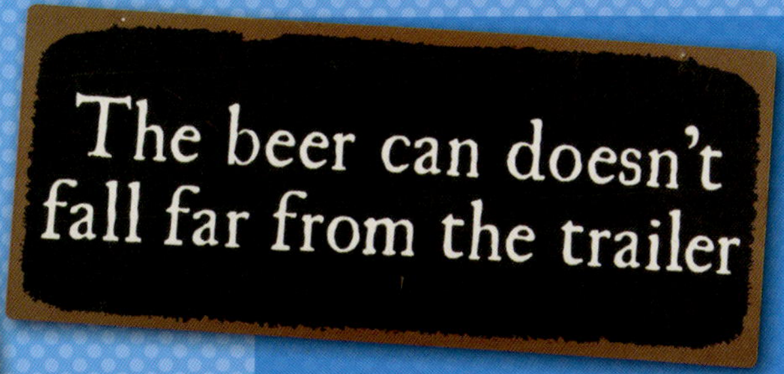

Old saying: "The beer can doesn't fall far from the trailer."
How eloquent! Modern metal sign, black and white, by Ohio Wholesale Inc., #33850, 14.25" x 6", c. 2010s. $10–$15

"Romany Gypsy Photograph Collection . . . 1939 Travelers Stop Overnight Near Leads" (England)

(On reverse side) Unused tourist postcard, black-and-white photo, from York, England, unnumbered, large 8" x 6", c. 2000s. This outstanding picture captures many of the details of real life in the early gypsy wagons, and it helps explain the historic background to the trailer trash label. $5–$10

"Het leven in Woonwagens."

Unused tourist postcard, black-and-white photo, no maker identified, #5480, 5.25" x 3.5", c. 1900s. Life in these early "mobile home" wagons provided basic shelter, but not much more. $10–$15

The dream mobile home cannot be complete without a pair of pink plastic flamingos!

Unused comic tourist postcard, color photo, by Zazzle, unnumbered, 5.5" x 4.25", c. 2010s. This scene is typical of the stereotype of trailer trash, right down to the cheap lawn chair and portable barbecue in the trailer's front yard. $5–$10

Early caravan comedy! "You don't need to eat with your knife–somebody will feed you in (my caravan)," and "There is plenty of pie in (my caravan)."

Two humorous tourist postcards, one used, one unused, by T. P. and Co., both from series #243, 5.5" x 3.5", one posted 1917 from/to Maryland (postmark and address illegible). We are not sure what impression these cards would have created. Would viewers have thought well of the nicely dressed couples in the attractive little house wagons, or would Victorian viewers have seen her as trailer trash, a temptress trying to lure him to her den? Each, $10–$15

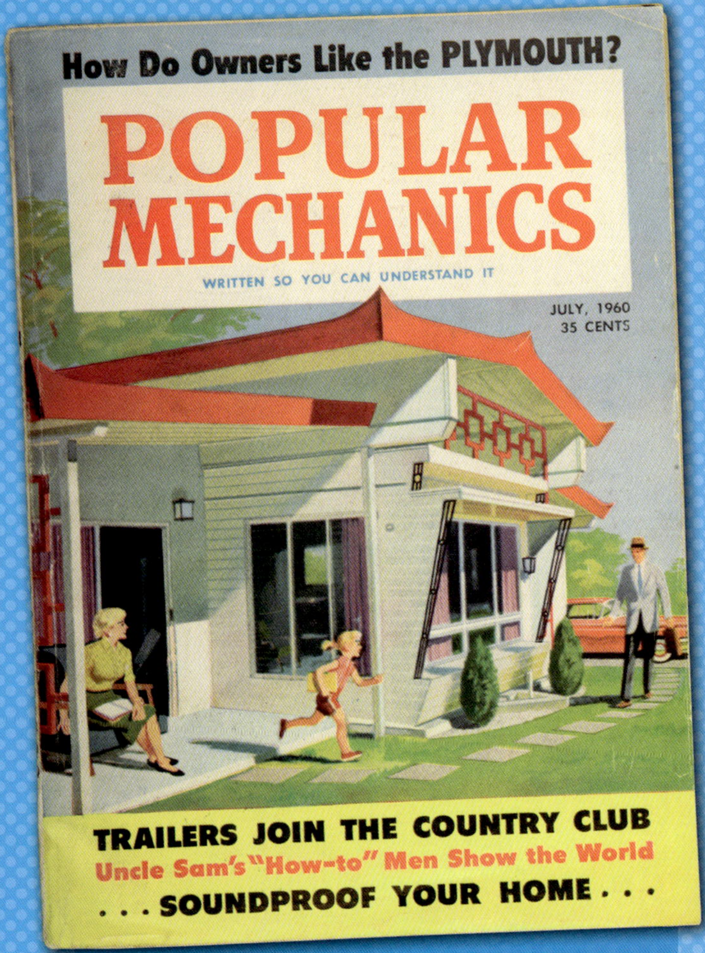

"Trailers Join The Country Club"

Elegant! Magazine article, in *Popular Mechanics*, July 1960, cover picture and page 94. The article observed: "Some fabulous things are happening, and mobile homes are becoming permanent and luxurious residences" (page 95). For the issue, $10–$15

"Blue Skies Trailer Village . . . America's Most Luxurious Trailer Park . . . Near Palm Springs, California"

(On reverse side) Unused advertising postcard, color photo, by Curteich, #6C-K959, 5.5" x 3.5", c. 1950s. The text described the residents of this upscale mobile home location: "It is the concept of Bing Crosby, President. . . . Co-habitues (and landlords) include Humphrey Bogart and Lauren Bacall, Jack Benny, Barbara Stanwyck, Danny Kaye, Greer Garson, George Burns and Gracie Allen, Jose Ferrer and Rosemary Clooney, Claudette Colbert, and many others." Wow! $10–$15

"Princeton Trailer Court . . . Tucson, Arizona"

(On reverse side) Unused advertising postcard, color photo, by Photocraft and Dexter Press, #79097, 5.5" x 3.5", c. 1950s. Wicked good site! This grand scene has everything a trailerite could hope for—a grand coach, manicured lawn, and picket fence. Indeed, the text on the card's back touts it as "Luxury Living." $15–$20

"Laguna Beach, California . . . Picturesque 'Treasure Isle' and Beautiful Treasure Island Trailer Park"

(Above) (On reverse side) Used advertising postcard, color photo, by George Watson and Colourpicture, unnumbered, 5.5" x 3.5", copyright 1954, posted to Hedrick, Iowa (postmark illegible). This location became a famous mobile home park, and was even shown briefly in the movie *The Long, Long Trailer.* $10–$15

"Ohio Deluxe Trailer Court . . . Sarasota, Florida"

(Below) (On reverse side) Unused advertising postcard, color photo, by Marvis Studio, #9176, 5.5" x 3.5", c. 1950s. Oh, the peace, quiet, and comfort. $10–$15

"Palisades Trailer Bowl . . . Santa Monica, Calif."

(Above) (On reverse side) Used advertising postcard, color photo, by Colourpicture, #P15524, 5.5" x 3.5", posted 1957 from Santa Monica, California, to Cleveland, Ohio. The text described this location as: "157 Terraced 'Ocean View' completely modern lots 'By The Beach'." Sounded like true paradise! $5–$10

"Mobile Home Section . . . Orange Blossom Hills Florida"

(Below) (On reverse side) Unused advertising postcard, color photo, by Dexter Color Illinois, #98342-B, 5.5" x 3.5", c. 1960s–1970s. It looked absolutely delightful! $5–$10

"Trailer Camp Friendships" by Douglass Crockwell and "In this friendly, freedom-loving land of ours-Beer belongs-enjoy it."

Magazine advertisement, in *Woman's Home Companion*, 10.5" x 13.5", c. 1940s. What an attractive and inviting patio scene for the leisure set around their mobile homes—complete with lawn furniture and a white picket fence! $5–$10

"Holiday Hills Mobile Home Resort . . . Denver, Colorado"

(On reverse side) Used advertising postcard, real color photo, by Colourpicture, unnumbered, 5.5" x 3.5", posted 1971 from Denver, Colorado, to Buffalo, New York. Colorful and appealing picture composition! $5–$10

"High Style by Henslee"

Used advertising postcard, color photo, by Quantity Postcards, unnumbered, 5.5" x 3.5", copyright 1986, posted 1993 to Topanga, California (postmark partially illegible). The text noted: "Leader in Quality Construction and Fine Interior Appointments." The image of this shiny, long, long coach looked almost glamorous with the model stepping out the doorway. $5–$10

"Federation of Mobile Home Owners of Florida, Inc."

Window decal, no maker identified, unnumbered, 4.75" x 3.25" oval, c. 1950s–1960s. A stately looking mobile home! $5–$10

"Beautiful Winter Haven Court" (Fairhope, Alabama)

(Above) Unused advertising postcard, color photo, by Stratis Photography and Dexter Press, 5.5" x 3.5", c. 1970s. The scene was really quite attractive! See the adjacent card from the very same mobile home location. $5–$10

"Beautiful Winter Haven Court" (Fairhope, Alabama)

(Below) Used advertising postcard, color photo, by Stratis Photography and Dexter Press, #51931-C, 5.5" x 3.5", posted 1973 from Fairhope, Alabama, to Phoenix, Arizona. This clever card's text on the reverse side asked its recipients to "retire with us." $5–$10

"It's time to move up with Bendix."

(On reverse side) Scarce cards! Two unused advertising postcards, architectural renderings, no makers identified, unnumbered, 6" x 4", c. 1960s. Both cards depict upscale and sizable Bendix mobile homes in floor plans ranging from about 1400 to 1750 square feet. Each, $10–$15

Let's Polka! "Lawrence Welk Country Club Village"

(On reverse side) Two unused advertising postcards, color photos, by Darby Photography, 5.5" x 3.5", c. 1960s–1970s. The card above showed the "front entrance of Lawrence Welk's Mobile Home," postcard #LW20 and #51660. The card below shows the "Champagne Glass Fountain" with high-end mobile homes in the background, postcard #LW22 and #51662. Each, $10–$15

"River Rose Mobile Homes" (Spokane, Washington)

Unused advertising postcards, color photos, by Commercial Photographers, #47425 and #51831, 5.5" x 3.5", c. 1950s–1960s. The text exclaimed: "Suburban Living . . . at its finest!" See the adjacent card as well. Each, $10–$15

"Pattern For . . . Smart Living . . . Trailer Coach Manufacturers Assn"

Magazine advertisement, black-and-white text with color pictures, full-page 10.75" x 13.74", c. 1950s. The text of this ad boasted that the purchase of a trailer house "buys every facility of a well-insulated, smartly furnished three-room home . . . It's a pattern more and more thousands are choosing!" $5–$10

Everybody out of your mobile homes! Pool party! "Trailer Life in the Desert"

(On reverse side) Unused tourist postcard, color photo, by Curteichcolor, #G-208 and #6C-K954, 5.5" x 3.5", c. 1950s. The text: "Many enjoy the benefits of relaxing in the desert sunshine in a number of attractive trailer parks that are to be found in this resort area." $5–$10

Oh, Britannia! "Luxury 33 Ft. Caravans . . . At Holimarine-Britain's Unique Holiday Village At Burnham-On-Sea In Glorious Somerset"

(On reverse side) Used advertising postcard, color photo, by Colourpicture Publishers, #P57546, 5.5" x 3.5", posted 1970 from Somerset to Kent, England. The senders wrote in their message on the back of the card: "The caravan on the postcard is the same as ours. It's super." It certainly looked comfortable. $5–$10

Outstanding card! "Marlette Coach Company, Marlette, Mich."

(On reverse side) Unused advertising postcard, artist's rendering, by Leshore Calgift Corp., #44,117F, 5.5" x 3.5", c. 1950s–1960s. The text on the reverse side touted: "Marlette offers the most in comfort, luxury and convenience." $15–$20

A mansion on wheels! "The Mobile Home . . . Mobile Homes Manufacturers Assn."

Magazine advertisement, color photo, full-page 10.5" x 13.75", c. 1950s–1960s. A note under the picture pointed out that the photograph of the upscale coach and its perfect landscaping was taken at "Better Mobile Home Park," Springfield, Massachusetts. No wonder the chapter is called "living like a millionaire." $5–$10

"Palm Coves . . . Palm Springs, Calif."

(On reverse side) Unused advertising postcard, color photo, by Dennis Holmes Photos and Dexter Press, #53781-B, 5.5" x 3.5", dated 1962. In the printed text, this location was described as "Luxury Estates For Mobile Homes." $5–$10

"Garden Valley Mobile Home Park . . . Colorado Springs, Colorado"

(On reverse side) Unused advertising postcard, color picture, by Douglas Smith, unnumbered, c. 1960s–1970s. This coach was blessed with near perfect landscaping! $5–$10

Fabulous find! "Take a peek at . . . Colonial for 1956."

Folding advertising brochure, black-and-white and color photos, by Colonial Coach Manufacturing Corporation, unnumbered, 8.5" x 11.5" folded (17" x 11.5" unfolded), dated 1956. This marvelous mid-century piece featured a glamorous lady introducing a stunning red and gray luxury mobile home—seemingly fit for a millionaire. $20–$25

"Embassy Mobile Home Park . . . Clearwater, Florida"

(On reverse side) Used advertising postcard, color photo, by Roger Luce and Dexter Press, #5654-C, 5.5" x 3.5", posted 1966 from Clearwater, Florida, to Fort Plain, New York. With the rose bushes, as pictured, this location seemed to be a park of the first magnitude, and the senders' handwritten note even mentioned: "The rose garden is back of the Recreation Hall." $5–$10

"The most wonderful mobile home life I have ever seen . . . the Mobile Home Park at Aldersgate Retiral Center, Kissimmee, Florida."

(On reverse side) Used advertising postcard, color photo, by Robert Wasman, #127375, 5.5" x 3.5", posted 1972 from Kissimmee, Florida, to Grove City, Ohio. What a restful, relaxing scene! Let's all retire! $5–$10

"Willow Trailer Park, Long Beach, California"

Unused advertising postcard, linen, two view, by E. B. Thomas, #E-11058, 5.5" x 3.5", c. 1940s. Catchy phrase printed on the back: "A Particular Park for Particular People." Also, the text claimed: "California's Finest New Deluxe and Modern Trailer Park." It certainly looked dreamy! $10–$15

"Southern Comfort Trailer Park . . . Clearwater, Florida"

(On reverse side) Unused advertising postcard, color photo, by Ward Beckett and Co., #C-16217, 5.5" x 3.5", c. 1950s. What a simple and stately picture! The text proclaimed: "Ideal, year-round retirement village." $5–$10

"Holiday Park Mobile Home Residential Villages . . . Port Charlotte, Florida"

(On reverse side) Used advertising postcard, color photo, by General Development Corp., #SA-5211-HP-0, 5.5" x 3.5", posted 1973 from/to Cleveland, Ohio. This low-key card's text spoke of "fresh start Florida living" and "attractive mobile home avenues." No hard sell here. $5–$10

"Orchard Trailer Villa, Palm Springs, California"

(On reverse side) Unused advertising postcard, color photo, by Ferris Scott and Western Resort Publications, #FS-98 and #S3781, 5.5" x 3.5", c. 1950s. Picture perfect upper crust living! But, with a folksy flair, here was part of the text: "One of Palm Springs most picturesque trailer villas where trailer life is enjoyed to the fullest. . . . Many trailer folk live a leisurely life of ease and comfort the year round." $10–$15

"We're Staying At Beautiful Paradise Park" (in "Chicagoland," Chicago Heights, Illinois)

Unused advertising postcard, color photo, by H. S. Crocker Co., unnumbered, 5.5" x 3.5", c. 1950s–1960s. According to the text on the card's back: "Most Beautiful—Spacious Mobile Home Facilities In The Midwest." $5–$10

"Citrus Haven Trailer Park . . . Phoenix, Arizona"

(On reverse side) Unused advertising postcard, color photo, by Bob Van Luchene and Petley Studios, #32122, 5.5" x 3.5", c. 1950s–1960s. This small, cozy location with only some thirty-five sites, according to the text on the card's reverse side, was "one of the Valley's most popular trailer resorts." It looks nice to us, too. $5–$10

"Sierra Dawn Estates" (Hemet, California)

Used advertising postcard, color photo, by Jack Kneass and Dexter Press, #63458-D, 5.5" x 3.5", posted 1964 from Murrieta to Culver City, California. The text on the reverse side called this location "America's finest mobile home subdivision." Can't beat that! $5–$10

"Home Sweet Home"

(On reverse side) Unused art postcard, from a painting by artist Paige Bridges, unnumbered, 5" x 4", c. 2000s. Complete with flowers and white picket fence, this home-site appears picture-perfect. $5–$10

"Palm Springs Travel Lodge Mobile Home Park" (Cathedral City, California)

(On reverse side) Unused advertising postcard, color photo, by Dennis Holmes and Dexter Press, #71441-B, 5.5" x 3.5", c. 1950s–1960s. The text: "Palm Spring's Newest De Luxe Park" (that's not our typo!). $5–$10

"Rodeo Court . . . Colorado Springs, Colo."

Used advertising postcard, chrome, by Douglas Smith and Tichnor, unnumbered, 5.5" x 3.5", posted 1959 from Colorado Springs, Colorado, to Chicago, Illinois. With the mountains in the background and the white picket fence and large striped awning outside the featured coach, the scene was impressive. $10–$15

Chapter 5

What's in a Name?

Is it a trailer house, house trailer, or mobile home? And then, what do we call a group of those homes on wheels? Not a flock, gaggle, or school. We often call it a mobile-home park—or better still, a mobile-home "resort," "lodge," "estate," "village," "manor," "court," or the like. The names can be very important, for it may set the tone and influence the reality for the mobile-home community.

A name can make a big difference. It's like curb appeal, a first impression. Often, the first thing seen or heard about something is its name. Besides, a good name can set the stage for positive perceptions, while the opposite effect can result from an undesirable name. In regard to mobile-home locations, names that include phrases such as "fish camp" or even "trailer park" create very different impressions than locations with names, such as "mobile home villa," or "mobile home harbor." You will see some creative and clever mobile home park names in this chapter.

Importantly, a degree of reality frequently accompanies an entity's name, as the choice of a business name may actually reflect its features and condition, or create an aspirational attitude about it. Concerning mobile-home sites, there is a wide array of differences from one to another—especially in regard to their sizes, services, configurations, and amenities. This chapter illustrates these variations, particularly their amenities, among better mobile-home locations.

Trailer Park Boys . . . The Movie.

Yahoo! Movie advertising card, 5.5" x 8", c. 2000s. Here, on this card and in the humorous film, you will find many of the current trailer trash stereotypes, starting with the crumpled and rusted 1961 license plate in the center of the card, to all of the adverse images of the subculture of low-end trailer parks in the comedic movie. $5–$10

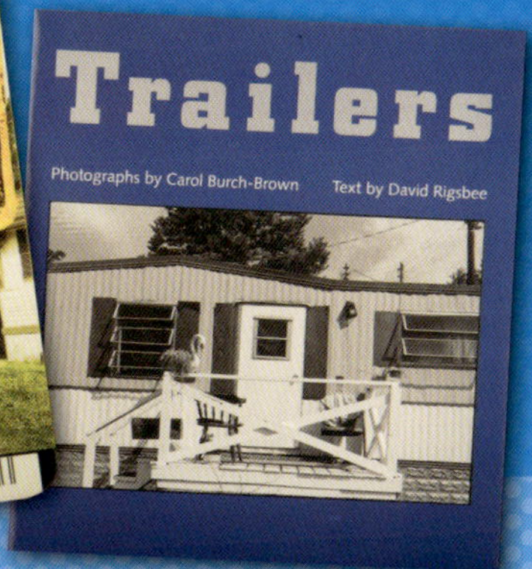

Trailers

Paperback book of text and black-and-white photographs by David Rigsbee and Carol Burch-Brown, 8" x 9", 93 pages, copyright 1996. An outstanding, must-see book for everyone seriously interested in the culture of the mobile home. The choice of the name "Trailers," suggests a particular view of the book's low-income and lower-end Appalachian examples. Although the book is a compassionate portrayal, there are no pictures of higher-end mobile homes or trailer-house communities. $20–$25

"Lattice Compound," "Tornado Bait," "Vertigo," "A Touch of Class," "Picket Fence and All," and "Lavender and Lattice"

Board game cards, from Trailer Park Wars game, 3.5" x 2.25", copyright 2007. These clever and fun game cards illustrate several trailer trash labels or names for the pictured mobile homes. We have other pieces from this entertaining board game elsewhere in the book. For the group, $5–$10

(On box) "SSS Toys . . . House Trailer"

Japan tin toy tow car and house trailer, with its original box, SSS brand, cardboard box 11" x 4.25" x 4", c. 1940s–1950s. In the early era of the development of true mobile homes, they were first called "house trailers" or "trailer houses"—at best, a most modest description. Rare toy find!!! $300-$400, including its outdoor tin patio furniture set (not shown).

Spectacular toy! Highly detailed! "House Trailer"

Japan tin toy trailer house, c. 1950s. Again, the name printed on the side of this vintage toy—"House Trailer"—was so broad that, in those early years, it was thought to include virtually every travel trailer, regardless of its small size, its usage, or its poor condition. This uniquely designed toy included a fully detailed interior (complete with black-and-white checkerboard floor pattern), a roof with transparent plastic windows (allowing for the viewing of the inside of the coach), and working/moving features, such as the side entry door, four wheels, and trailer hitch. $200-$250

"Walt Disney's Mickey Mouse Club . . . Mobile Home Picture Puzzle"

Amazing graphics! Jigsaw puzzle, by Jaymar, #139, 100+ pieces, 18" x 13", c. 1960s. Importantly, the tiny 1930s era "canned-ham" travel trailer pictured here was called a "mobile home." So, the cramped conditions, with laundry drying on the roof, became the image of a mobile home—apparently according to one of the most trusted of all possible sources: Walt Disney Studios. $15–$20

"Newt's . . . Exclusive Trailer Park . . . St. Augustine, Fla."

(On reverse side) Can there be any higher designation than "exclusive" for a mobile home site? Used (but not posted) advertising postcard, color photo, two view, by R. A. Lasater, #67584, 5.5" x 3.5", dated 1967. According to the printed text: "New 10 wide Mobile Homes for rent." $5–$10

"Horseshoe Trailer Villa" (El Cajon, California)

Used advertising postcard, linen, by Nationwide Specialty, unnumbered, 5.5" x 3.5", posted 1953 from San Diego to Lawndale, California. "Villa" was a savvy name selection. The sender of this card concluded her message: "This is a pretty trailer park." $10–$15

"A Home-Dream Come True!"

Magazine advertisement, *Saturday Evening Post*, 10.5" x 13.75", March 9, 1946. Notice the reference to the post World War II national housing difficulty: "Housing Shortage Relieved With Trailer Coaches …" It was dreamy! The text boasted: "You'll be amazed at the comfort, convenience and efficiency built into these mobile homes …" But, also note the absence of a bathroom in the cutaway view of the pictured dream coach. $10–$15

"Kountry Klub Trailer Park . . . Abilene, Texas"

(Above) Unused advertising postcard, black-and-white aerial photo, by United Ayr Vues, #1m-154-6, 5.5" x 3.5", c. 1950s–1960s. Interestingly, this card includes the only reference we have seen to one of the common concerns about mobile home park living—the availability of a "storm cellar." $5–$10

"Country Club Park With Great Mobile Home Living" (Wickenburg, Arizona)

(Below) (On reverse side) Unused advertising postcard, color photo, by Bill Bass and McGrew Printing, #615650, 5.5" x 3.5", c. 1960s–1970s. The picture looked like a country club setting. We especially enjoyed this part of the card's printed text: "Relaxation here means the rest of your life." *Hmmmm . . .* $5–$10

"Shangri-La . . . Largo, Florida"

(Above) (On reverse side) Classy rec hall! Used advertising postcard, color photo, by Ward Beckett, #70890, 5.5" x 3.5", posted 1966 from Largo, Florida, to Levittown, Pennsylvania. The text called this location "one of the nation's finest mobile home parks," for "country club living." $5–$10

"Shangri La Mobile Home Park . . . Lakeland, Florida"

(Below) (On reverse side) Used advertising postcard, color aerial photo, by Punta Gorda Postcard and Dukane Press, #5073, 5.5" x 3.5", posted 1973 from Lakeland, Florida, to Delmar, Delaware. This catchy slogan appeared in the card's text: "Small enough to know you. Big enough to serve you." $5–$10

"Johnie Cleveland's Trailer Town" (near Jackson, Mississippi)

(On reverse side) Used advertising postcard, color photo, by Bob Hand and Dexter Press, #64028-C, 5.5" x 3.5", posted 1971 from Georgia to Cuyahoga Falls, Ohio. With some 160 mobile home sites, this "Trailer Town" probably would have had a small-town atmosphere—with a large outdoor swimming pool and with about one-third more sites than claimed on the next card. $5–$10

"Johnie Cleveland's Trailer Town" (near Jackson, Mississippi)

(On reverse side) Used advertising postcard, color photo, by MWM Co., #43,784F, 5.5" x 3.5", posted 1966 from Jackson, Mississippi, to St. Petersburg, Florida. The text on this postcard referred to "110 lots," rather than to the 160 sites mentioned by the preceding card. The senders in their handwritten message remarked that they "just went swimming in this pool." A pool is a very important amenity! $5–$10

"We've retired to a life of ease with our Mobile Home in Florida! . . . College Park Mobile Homes, Orlando, Fla."

Magazine advertisement, black-and-white photos, in *National Geographic*, 6.5" x 10", dated 1954. Notice the price tag for a new coach—"from $2000 to $6000." And, that price included furnishings! $5–$10

"Valley Rancho Trailer Park . . . LaVerne, California"

(On reverse side) Used advertising postcard, color photo, two view, by Frasbers, Inc., #18385, 5.5" x 3.5", posted 1960 from LaVerne, California, to St. Helens, Oregon. This was a relatively small and charming location, as the colorful picture and text pointed out: "With 71 large spaces, large trees and a country atmosphere." $10–$15

"Goforth Mobile Home Village . . . Orange, California"

(On reverse side) Upper crust atmosphere! Unused advertising postcard, color photo, by Sorensen Photography and Smart Studio, #46323 and #KE2-3603, 3.5" x 5.5", c. 1960s. The description in the text read: "Tropical setting surrounded by orange and palm trees. Beautiful recreation building with heated and filtered pool." $5–$10

Let the games begin! " Sarasota Mobile Home Park" (Florida)

(On reverse side) Used advertising postcard, color photo, by Florida Pre-Vues, #7046, 5.5" x 3.5", posted 1959 from Sarasota, Florida, to Chillicothe, Ohio. This location was owned and operated by the city, and the card's picture shows a happy day on the park's shuffleboard courts. And, the senders' handwritten message, not surprisingly, declared, "this Florida life is for us." $5–$10

"Bella-Vista Mobile Homes Lodge" (Cayucos, California)

Unused advertising postcard, color aerial photo by Carl Schultz, #S30744, 5.5" x 3.5", c. 1960s. This location claimed to be: "The finest mobile home in all central California." $5–$10

Handsome vintage card! "Shuffleboard at Bradenton Trailer Park, Bradenton, Fla."

Used advertising postcard, linen, by Curteich, #B-16 and #6B-H2640, 5.5" x 3.5", posted 1948 from Bradenton, Florida, to Perth Amboy, New Jersey. The sender's handwritten message was emphatic: "This is the life for me." $10–$15

"Marina Mobile Estates" (Thermal, California)

An "estate" is an upper-crust place. Unused advertising postcard, color aerial photo, by Bert Lang and Dexter Press, #7731-C, 5.5" x 3.5", 1950s–1960s. The text on the back of this card proudly declared: "The only park west of Florida where each mobile home has its own water frontage and dock space." $5–$10

"Holiday Spa Mobile Home Resort . . . Phoenix, Arizona"

(On reverse side) "Resort" carries a strong upscale ring to it. Unused advertising postcard, color aerial photo, by Henry McGrew Printing, #33850, 5.5" x 3.5", c. 1960s. The unique text on the card boasted: "Featuring $250,000 Clubhouse . . . 333 Deluxe Spaces . . . 'Where everyday is a Holiday.'" $5–$10

"Parkway Mobile Home Village" (Sandusky, Ohio)

Unused advertising postcard, color photo, by Grauer Photographic Art, #46472, 5.5" x 3.5", c. 1970s. $5–$10

"Nut Tree Mobile Estates" (Beaverton, Oregon)

Unused advertising postcard, color photo, three view, by Gan Advertising and Dexter Press, #49160-B, 5.5" x 3.5", c. 1950s–1960s. According to the text: "One of the newest and most modern Trailer parks in the Portland area." $5–$10

Great swimming pools and spa scene! "Good Life Travel Trailer Resort . . . Mesa, Arizona"

(On reverse side) Unused advertising postcard, color photo, two view, no maker identified, unnumbered, 3.5" x 5.5", c. 1980s. It appears from the row of mobile homes shown in the upper picture, that many coaches at this upscale resort do not travel at all. We would not venture away either after reading the tempting description in the text: "Where the good life is all that you want it to be . . . under swaying palms in the magical Southwest." $5–$10

"Cottonwood Cove . . . Lake Mohave of the Colorado River . . . Searchlight, Nevada"

(On reverse side) Spectacular setting for the mobile homes pictured here! Unused advertising postcard, color aerial photo, by Norm's Publishing and Dexter Press, #56402-B, 5.5" x 3.5", c. 1960s. $5–$10

Ahoy! Caption "Myakka River Manor Mobilehome Park . . . Venice, Fla."

(On reverse side) One could not aspire to much more than a "manor" in Venice! Used advertising postcard, color photo, no maker identified, #491072, 5.5" x 3.5", posted 1974 from Venice, Florida, to Huntington, Indiana. What a dreamy waterfront setting! $10–$15

Indiana "MBL HM DLR" (Mobile Home Dealer) license plate, 1993.

It is quite unusual to find a mobile home dealer plate! $25–$30

"Mobile Home."

(On reverse side) Unused comic tourist card, color photo, by Gregory Thorp and Palm Press, #P0011, 6" x 4.25", photo dated 1992/card dated 1994. This building, clad in used license plates, is truly a "mobile home." See the next 21 images! $10–$15

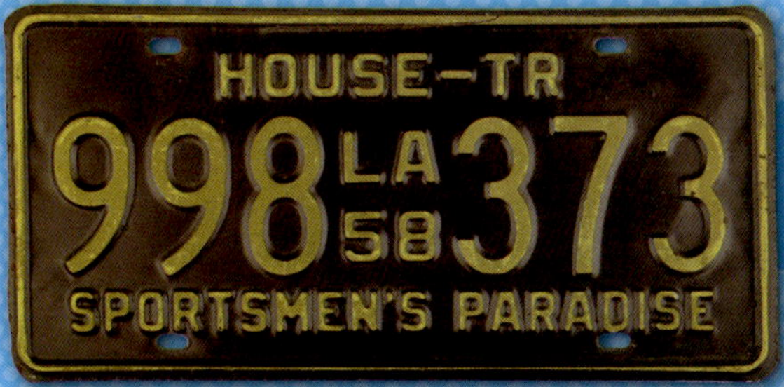

Louisiana "HOUSE TR" (Trailer) license plate, 1958.

Great vintage plate! $20–$25

New Mexico "MH MANUFACTURED HOME"

License plate, c. 2000s. $15–$20

Ohio "HOUSE VEH" (Vehicle) license plate, 1961.

Ohio may be the only state to have issued "House Vehicle" license plates. $20–$25

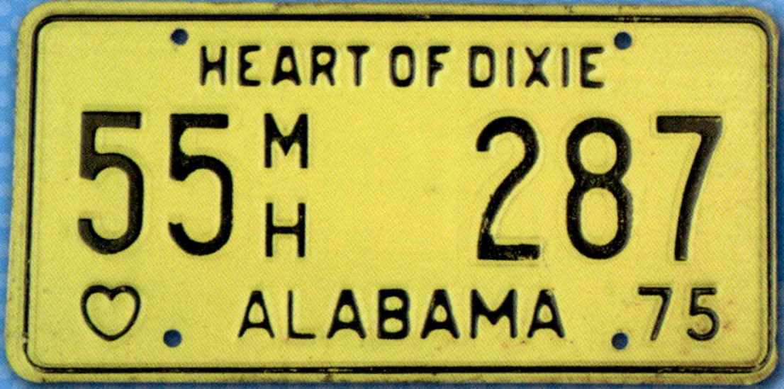

Alabama "MH" (Mobile Home)
License plate, 1975. $10–$15

Arizona "M-H" (Mobile Home)
License plate, 1973. $10–$15

Arkansas "MOBILE HOME"
License plate, c. 1970s–1980s. $10–$15

Colorado "MOB (MOBILE) HOME"
License plate, 1962. $15–$20

Florida "MH" (Mobile Home)
License plate, 1966. $10–$15

Idaho "HOUSE TRAILER"
License plate, c. 1970s–1980s. $10–$15

Iowa "MOBILE HOME"
License plate, c. 1970s–1980s. $10–$15

Minnesota "MOBL (MOBILE) HOME"
License plate, 1965. $15–$20

Kentucky "HT HOUSE TRAILER"
License plate, 1972. $10–$15

Nebraska "MOBL (MOBILE) HOME"
License plate, c. 1970s–1980s. $10–$15

North Dakota 'MOBILE HOME"
License plate, 1958. $10–$15

Oklahoma "HOUSE TRAILER"
License plate, 1965. $10–$15

Oklahoma "MOBILE HOME"
License plate, 1973. $10–$15

Tennessee "MOBILE HOME"
License plate, 1966. $10–$15

Texas "HOUSE TRAILER"
License plate, 1970. $10–$15

Texas "MOBILE HOME"
License plate, 1980. $10–$15

Wisconsin "MH MOBILE HOME"
License plate, 1992. $10–$15

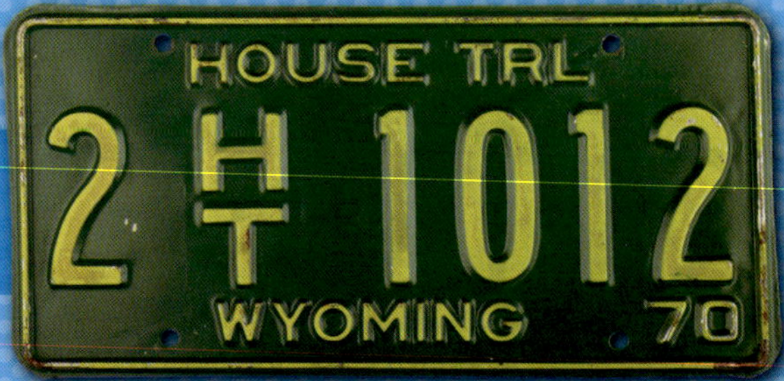

Wyoming "HT HOUSE TRL (Trailer)"
License plate, 1970. $10–$15

Chapter 6

Water, Water, Everywhere

Water is a mobile home's best friend . . . and its worst enemy. Almost all mobile-home owners prefer their coaches near an ocean, lake, or river—or at least to have a water view or a swimming pool. But, too much water is really bad for mobile homes, which (like cars, trucks, and RVs) tend to float for a while if floods develop.

As should be expected by now, water problems of some kind will almost certainly contribute to the trailer trash stereotype about mobile-home living—whether it's plumbing and sewer issues, rain and roof leaks, or flood waters. Even water mishaps associated with mobile-home swimming pools and spas can contribute to the image.

What is the real story about water and most mobile homes? Mobile homes with waterfront footage, water access, and/or water views are almost always more valuable. So, some mobile-home parks are built along canals, rivers, lakes, and even oceans. Remember also that fishing is an extremely popular pastime. Some mobiles are located to allow for on-site boat dockage—sometimes right at individual residences. Most certainly, swimming pools—either pools for individual residences, or community pools—are expected. As you will see, this chapter contains many images of upscale mobile-home parks near bodies of water and having appealing swimming pools.

"Trailer Park . . . Camping . . . Fishing" (On the background sign)

Unused tourist postcard, black-and-white photo, no maker identified, unnumbered, 3.5" x 5.5", c. 1930s–1940s. The proud couple pictured here had reeled in a big fish, at least three to four feet long. Many early waterfront and water-access mobile home and travel trailer parks were called "fish camps," because of the popularity of fishing and boating that attracted residents and visitors. But many of those places were decidedly low-end facilities that contributed to the trailer trash stereotype. And still today, if one wants to direct a barb at a mobile home resort, one needs only to refer to it as a fish camp. $10–$15

"Black Hills Flood Disaster . . . June 9, 1972"

(On reverse side) Unused tourist postcard, color aerial photo, by Kluge Industries, #K1, 5.5" x 3.5", dated 1972. The text on the back noted: "Aerial picture shows pile-up of mobile homes, near Campbell Street, in Rapid City, So. Dakota." Unfortunately, when flooding occurs, mobile homes behave somewhat like boats, and tend to float around—at least for brief periods. $10–$15

"Where Good Fishing Is Guaranteed . . . Guernsey City Tampa, Fla."

The text on the back boasted: "Officially rated the nation's finest mobile home retirement village." Unused advertising postcard, color photo, by W. R. Marion, #44122, 5.5" x 3.5", c. 1950s–1960s. $10–$15

(In French) "Boulogne-Sur-Mer-L'Heure du Bain."

Unused tourist postcard, black-and-white photo, no maker identified, #99, 5.5" x 3.5", c. 1900s. These early beach houses on wheels served as one of many early roll models for what developed into the modern mobile home. It seems so incongruous that these tiny beach houses that were rolled into the water contributed to the creation of mobile homes, which are so vulnerable to flood waters. See the next card as well. $20–$25

Rare find!

Used international tourist postcard, no maker identified, unnumbered, 5.5" x 3.5", posted 1909 from Missoula, Montana, to Monona, Iowa. This artistic rendering showed another view of these early mobile beach houses. $15–$20

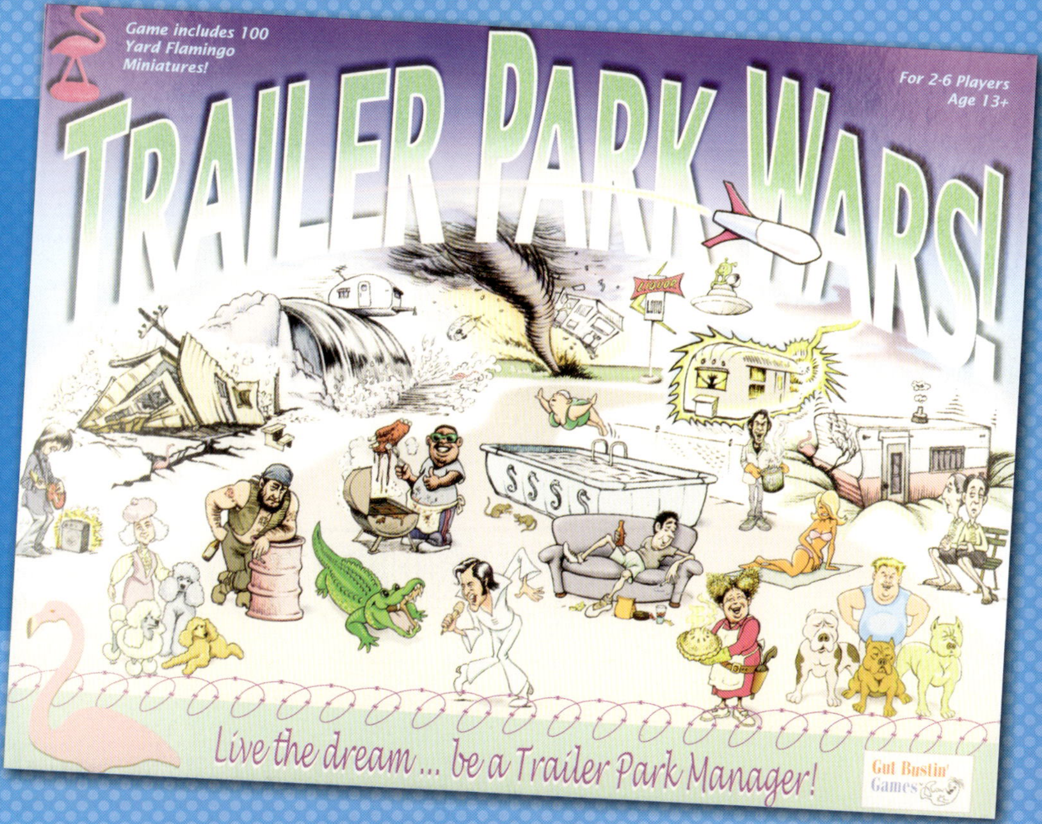

"Trailer Park Wars! . . . Live the dream . . . Be a Trailer Park Manager!"

Boxed game (box cover) , by Gut Bustin' Games, box 12.25" x 9.75" x 2", copyright 2007. Notice the image on the box cover of a small trailer being swept away by flood waters. This humorous game includes references to most of the barbs and comparisons that have contributed to the lasting influence of the trailer trash stereotype. It's terrific! For the complete boxed game, $20–$25

Spectacular imagery! A floating mobile home!

Numerous trailer owners have converted their coaches to floating houses by attaching them to pontoons or barges. Actually, standard house boats are forms of mobile homes, because they can move about on waterways and people can and do live in them. Entitled: "Cruising By Airstream." Print of multi-color painting by artist Bob Meredith, unnumbered, 13" x 8.5", 2009. Incidentally, notice how the artist showed the other trailers parked along the water's edge in this creative and colorful work. This print is displayed prominently in our home. $30–$40

"Mitchell Camp Mobile Home Park" (near Palo Verde, California)

(On reverse side) Unused advertising postcard, color photo, by Kendall Photography and Dexter Press, #11190-D, 3.5" x 5.5", c. 1970s–1980s. The text noted: "Ideal spot for retirement, fishing and camping." $5–$10

"Sewer Back-up!" "Flash Flood!!" "Glurrrp!! Jello in the Water Feature!"

Game cards, cardboard, 2.25" x 3.5", from Trailer Park Wars game, by Gut Bustin' Games, dated 2007. For the complete boxed game, $20–$25

"Me and the little woman hope you have a full Holiday Season."

The fun text on the back of the card continued: "And a New Year flush with good luck, good fortune, and good times!" Used holiday postcard, color graphics, homemade by our dear RV friends Fanny and Bill from Louisville, 5.5" x 4.25", posted 2013 from Louisville, Kentucky, to Eagle Lake, Florida. Undoubtedly, one of the most recent iconic displays of the trailer trash stereotype, without ever using that phrase, appeared in Chevy Chase's hit movie *National Lampoon's Christmas Vacation*, from which the idea for this clever card was conjured up. The pictured scene is of Uncle Eddie emptying the "sewer" (as this is a family-oriented book, we cannot use the word Eddie actually used in the movie to describe his activity) of his rather used mobile home that, to the dismay of the Griswold family, was parked in their front yard. As with stick-built houses, mobile home sewer issues can be real problems. See the next images as well. $10–$15

"Uncle Eddie's RV . . . National Lampoon's Christmas Vacation . . . Snow Village"

Two Christmas novelty decorations, small piece about 4.75" x 3.5" x 2.75", large box 10.75" x 5.75" x 4.5". Uncle Eddie figurine and miniature RV (lighted, too), by Department 56, #4030734, copyright 2013. The ultimate, legendary representation of trailer trash! Here, Uncle Eddie is emptying the sewer. $100–$125

Isn't it just grand to live in a mobile home with its own private swimming pool?!

(On reverse side) "In every setting the magnificent new Fleetwood Broadmore Custom is an outstanding example of modern mobile home engineering and design." Unused advertising postcard, color photo, by Color Card Corp., #69430-B, 5.5" x 3.5", c. 1960s. The text went on to point out the availability of "12 models, 42' to 55' in length." $10–$15

"Bermuda Garden Trailer Park . . . Tucson, Arizona"

(On reverse side) Unused advertising postcard, color photo, by Otto Done and Dexter Press, #34530-B, 3.5" x 5.5", c. 1950s. Spectacular image of the large mobile homes lined up near the lovely pool and flowering Oleander bushes! $10–$15

"Biltmore Gardens Trailer Park . . . Miami, Florida"

(On reverse side) Serene pool scene! Unused advertising postcard, color photo, by Colourpicture Publishers, #P8649, 5.5" x 3.5", c. 1960s. Here is another upscale description in this card's printed text: "A distinctive residence for dwellers in mobile homes." $5–$10

"Greetings from Cathedral City, California."

(Above) Fabulous composition! Unused advertising postcard, color photo, by Ferris Scott and Western Resort Publications, #FS–126 and #S–4535L3, 5.5" x 3.5", c. 1960s. The text: "When the eastern states are shivering in sub-zero temperatures, these desert winter guests are enjoying the warm waters of the Delux Trailer Park pool, and real desert living under a warm desert sun." Hallelujah! $10–$15

"LaPlaza Mobile Home Park . . . Just A Nice Place To Live . . . Clearwater, Florida"

(Below) (On reverse side) Used advertising postcard, black-and-white photo, no maker identified, unnumbered, 5.5" x 3.5", posted 1962 from Tampa, Florida, to Portersville, Pennsylvania. The senders drew a circle around the mobile home on the left side of this picture, and wrote the words "our house." The swimming pool, with its outdoor furniture and umbrella, seems to be an inviting feature. $10–$15

"This is typical of the luxurious waterfront Mobile Homes situated on the West Coast of Florida."

(On reverse side) Used tourist postcard, color photo, by Tropical Cards, #S–76122, 5.5" x 3.5", posted 1972 from Fort Myers, Florida, to Gladstone, Michigan. What a bonus it is to have a canal-front location! The senders of this card wrote a brief description of their mobile home setting: "Finally found a card somewhat like where we are staying. Trailer front faces the river canal. All lots are doubled, so it's not crowded at all." $5–$10

"Spring Lakes . . . in Scotts Valley . . . Santa Cruz, Calif."

(On reverse side) Lovely, lovely! Unused advertising postcard, color photo, by Scotts Valley Photography and Mike Roberts, #SC13158, 5.5" x 3.5", 1970s. This compelling description appeared in the card's printed text: "Set in a country club atmosphere on the sunny side of Santa Cruz, Spring Lakes represents the ultimate in design, setting and recreational facilities for Mobile Home living." $5–$10

"For carefree retirement-we chose a Mobile Home and sunny Arizona."

And, close to a handsome swimming pool! Magazine advertisement, black-and-white photos, 6.75" x 10", in *National Geographic*, c. 1950s. Even cowgirls and cowboys can be tamed into mobile home living. $5–$10

"Rainbow Isles . . . Exclusive Trailer Community . . . Pompano Beach, Florida"

(Above) (On reverse side) Used advertising postcard, color photo, by F. W. Sauer, #68291, 5.5" x 3.5" , posted 1964 from Fort Lauderdale, Florida, to Columbus, Ohio. The text on the back boasted that its park provided "the utmost in Mobile Home Living. Shuffleboard, swimming pool, and putting green. Fishing from your trailer. Select adult clientele." Just perfect—with all that water! $5–$10

"Bay Pines Park . . . St. Petersburg, Fla."

(Below) (On reverse side) Used advertising postcard, color photo, by Ward Beckett and Co., #133693, 5.5" x 3.5", posted 1974 from St. Petersburg, Florida, to Fairland, Indiana. The text on the reverse side pointed out: "Over 500 spaces on 3 private stocked lakes, in a shaded tropical setting . . . One of Florida West Coast's largest privately owned mobile home parks." What an ideal setting right on the water! $5–$10

"Tip-O-Texas RV Village . . . Pharr, Texas"

(Above) (On reverse side) Used advertising postcard, color aerial photo, by Southwest Commercial Printers, unnumbered, 6" x 4", posted 1986 from Texas to Muskegon, Michigan (postmark partially illegible). Even with some 860 sites in this park, the senders' message spoke of the location being full with folks spending the season—as many large RVs and mobile homes are used by winter seasonal residents in the southern USA. Notice the large pool and spa pictured here. $5–$10

"Lough Erne Holidays Caravan Site"

(Below) (On reverse side) Used advertising postcard, color photo, by Ranscombe Photographics, #NI556, 5.5" x 3.5", posted 1970 from Ireland to England. The text on the reverse emphasized the park's water access and the "numerous wooded islands . . . excellent fishing and water sporting activities." Several small sailboats can be seen in the center of the picture, with numerous large caravans (mobile homes) in the background. $5–$10

"Take One New Moon Home . . . Add Water And Enjoy Instant Vacation Living . . . New Moon Homes, Dallas, Texas"

It's the thesis of this chapter! Magazine advertisement, color photo, 5" x 11", in *Sports Afield*, May 1965, page 135. $5–$10

"Del Rio Trailer Park . . . Bell, Calif."

Unused advertising postcard, linen, by Colourpicture, #K5795, 5.5" x 3.5", c. 1940s. This time period was during the era when almost all house trailers were smaller and did not have inside bathrooms, so the text on the card referenced "125 beautiful landscaped spaces" and "36 tile showers," a good ratio of about one shower to every four sites. And, there was a handsome pool. $10–$15

"Canal Point Trailer Park and Sales . . . Fort Myers Beach, Fla."

(On reverse side) Unused advertising postcard, color aerial photo, by Punta Gorda Postcard, #26352, 5.5" x 3.5", c. 1960s. The printed text: "Offering waterfront spaces for mobile homes . . . new and used mobile homes available for sale or rent." $5–$10

"Green Acres Mobilehome Park . . . Clearwater, Florida."

(On reverse side) Unused advertising postcard, color photo, by Ward Beckett, #C-16221, 5.5" x 3.5", c. 1950s. Notice the festive pink and white mobile home setting at the left side of the attractive pool. The text pointed out that this park even had "illuminated shuffleboard courts" for that late-night entertainment. Yahoo! $5–$10

"Valle Vista Mobile Home Park, Hemet, Calif."

(On reverse side) Unused advertising postcard, color photo, by Mike Roberts and Valley Studios, #SC8052, 5.5" x 3.5", c. 1950s. The text described the location: "In 'The Foothills of Heaven'." $5–$10

"Sunset Mobile Home Park" (Pinellas Park, Florida)

Unused advertising postcard, color photos, three view, by MWM Co., #147,044, 5.5" x 3.5", c. 1980s. An impressive pool scene! $5–$10

"Garden Valley Mobile Home Park . . . Colorado Springs, Colorado"

(On reverse side) Unused advertising postcard, color photos, two view, by Douglas Smith, #090404. 5.5" x 3.5", c. 1970s. The combination of swimming pools and young women in bikinis must have seemed good for business. $5–$10

"Palm Trailer Park . . . Phoenix, Ariz."

(On reverse side) Used (but not mailed) advertising postcard, color photo, by Chase's Studio and Dexter Press, #95751, 5.5" x 3.5", c. 1950s. The swimming pool is often the central attraction at these hot-weather locations. $5–$10

"Deep Lagoon Mobile Park . . . New Port Richey, Florida."

(On reverse side) Unused advertising postcard, color photos, two view, by Florida Litho Co., #S17863, 5.5" x 3.5", c. 1950s. What a wonderful rainbow of mobile home colors! And, right on the water. The card's text claimed: "Florida's finest mobile home park." $10–$15

"Wagner Trailer Park . . . Desert Hot Springs, Calif."

(On reverse side) Unused advertising postcard, color photo, by Michael Hampton and Barnes Studio, #41675, 5.5" x 3.5", c. 1960s. This unique location, according to the card's text, provided: "The most luxurious park for Mobile Homes in the desert area offering therapeutic mineral water bathing. Two 132° natural hot-water mineral wells serve four therapeutic pools and a 25' x 50' swimming pool." How wonderful! $5–$10

"Country Club Mobile Homes Inc." (Yuma, Arizona)

Used advertising postcard, color aerial photo, by Art Fszol and Peg-Art Productions, #S-34147L2, 5.5" x 3.5", posted 1964 from Howard City, Michigan, to Lakeville, Indiana (and the handwritten note on the postcard indicated the senders had just arrived home from vacation when they sent this card). The pool pictured here would be a necessity in Arizona! $5–$10

"The Mobile Home Address of Distinction . . . Brentwood Park . . . Chula Vista, California . . . The Ultimate In Country Club Living"

(On reverse side) Used advertising postcard, color photo, by Amescolor Publishers, #49491, 5.5" x 3.5", posted 1961 from Inglewood, California, to Chiloquin, Oregon. The text on the back pointed out the "sparkling, heated, filtered pool" pictured on the front of the card. $5–$10

"Cherokee Mobile Home Park . . . Ft. Lauderdale, Fla."

(On reverse side) Unused advertising postcard, color photo, by Neel Color Cards, #37971, 5.5" x 3.5", 1950s–1960s. Every Florida location needs a pool, and the text on the card said this was a "new swimming pool." $5–$10

Chapter 7

Bringing What's Outside In

One of the major sources of ammunition for trailer trash attacks on mobile homes has been the perception about the undesirable things sometimes seen around the outside of mobile homes—people, animals, and junk. Presumably, those things must have either originated inside the mobile homes or should at least return to those coaches. Those outside things are the "trash" in trailer trash.

Ordinarily, "bringing the outdoors in" is a desirable goal. Builders of standard houses and interior designers are fond of planning elements intended to open up residential units to fresh air and the great outdoors (thereby effectively expanding the size of the basic housing structures and increasing their property values). Such elements could be included in the initial construction or could be added later.

Quality mobile-home residences are no different in this regard. Mobile homes can incorporate features like patios, screen rooms, and decks to open them up and to expand their square footages—as well as other standard mobile-home elements, such as awnings, roof-overs, and storage sheds. You will see numerous images relating to these various mobile home upgrades in this chapter. It's about bringing what's outside in—bringing in good things, not nasty things that are so exaggerated by trailer trash bashing.

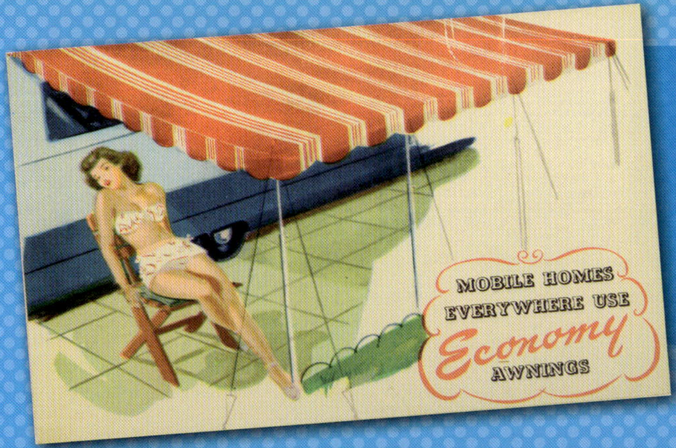

"Mobile Homes Everywhere Use Economy Awnings."
Yahoo! Fun and rare card! Unused advertising postcard, by Martin and Hoffman, unnumbered, 5.5" x 3.5", c. 1950s. There are several examples in this book of well-intentioned vendors in the mobile-home industry that may have contributed somewhat to the trailer trash stigma due to the images they employed in their advertising. See the next item. $20–$25

"Globemaster Mobile Homes, Inc., Goshen, Indiana"

Unused deck of 54 standard playing cards, real photo, 2.5" x 3.75", c. 1960s. Here again is an instance where this mobile-home advertising may have actually fostered the trailer trash image. $10–$15

(Translation of the French) "Those asses are showing off."

Unused comic tourist postcard, signed Bozz, published in Paris, France, 6" x 4", dated 1973. Notice the bikini-clad lady out on the balcony of the palatial two-story mobile home. Wonderful humor! $15–$20

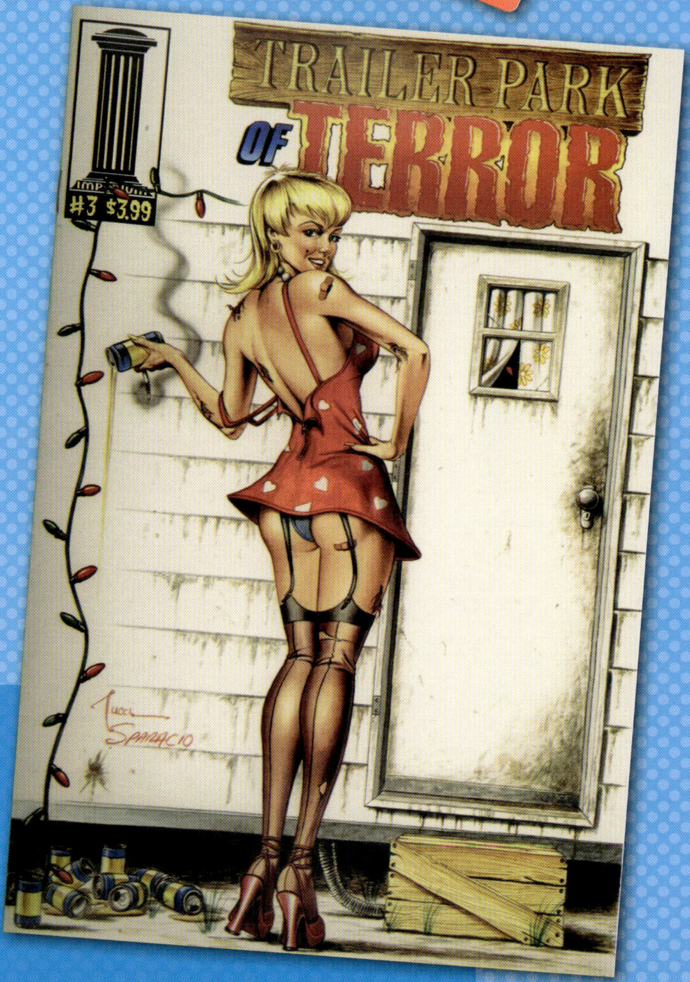

Trailer Park of Terror

Comic book, Color Special #3, by Imperium Comics, 6.5" x 10.25", thirty-six pages, June 2005. Fabulous stereotypic graphic of a mobile home and the scantily dressed lady from outside seeking to get inside. Notice the wooden crate entry step, the year-round Christmas lights, the sewer hose dangling under the coach, and the several beer cans laying on the ground. Picture perfect! $10–$15

"Herbert, Can't You See That The Bucket Has Over-Flowed?"

(Above) Unused humorous tourist postcard, by Trowel Publishing (England), #171, 5.5" x 3.5", c. 1940s. In the era of this card, British caravans did not yet have self-contained bathrooms, so much fun was poked at the use of outhouses—as was the case here. $10–$15

"All Set To Go Places And Do Things!"

(Below) Unused humorous tourist postcard, black-and-white photo, by L. L. Cook Co, #12X, 5.5" x 3.5", copyright 1938. Note the two outhouses labeled "MA" and "PA" being towed behind the handsome house trailer. These two comic postcards certainly promoted the trailer trash notion, without using the phrase. $10–$15.

"Interior of Gipsy Vardo about 1880 . . . West Yorkshire Folk Museum"

(On reverse side) Unused tourist postcard, color photo, by Richardson Printers (England), #C4, 4" x 6", c. 1940s. Wonderful view of an early gypsy caravan, showing the ornate, but cozy (cramped), quarters in which people lived. $10–$15.

Delicate landscape work at the mobile-home park.

Unused tourist postcard, black-and-white photo, no maker identified, unnumbered, 5.5" x 3.5", c. 1950s. We wonder how much of this mess will end up being tracked into the mobile home. $10–$15

Remarkable find! "Eccles Motor Caravans . . . Costa Green . . . Birmingham (England) . . . 8 Ft. Model . . . To Trail Behind Light Car And To Sleep Two Adults and One Child."

Can you believe it? It is so compact! Unused advertising postcard, black-and-white photos, five view, no maker identified, #15, large scale 5.25" x 7", c. 1920s. The five pictures on this marvelous old card displayed the great ingenuity of the manufacturer of this early trailer—showing, for instance, hinged/folding seats that became beds, under-seat storage lockers, hinged washbowl and tables, and shelving and cabinets. Before this time frame, either a tent or horse-drawn wagon with some outdoor equipment would have been the method of living while traveling. $25–$30

"Caravans For Hire Ltd . . . Birmingham" (England)

(On reverse side) Unused advertising postcard, black-and-white photo, by K Ltd (England), unnumbered, 3.5" x 5.5", c. 1920s. Illustrating how much can be crammed into the narrow space in early British caravans. Notice the overhead storage cabinets, the dishes strapped in place in the upper right corner, and the trolley roof design, which allowed for head-room down the center of the caravan where people would stand. Rare card. $15–$20

"Interior of Caravan 'Walden' . . . From Bertram Hutchings, Winchester" (England)

Scarce find! Unused tourist postcard, black-and-white photo, no maker identified, unnumbered, 5.5" x 3.5", c. 1930s. Here, a slightly larger caravan's furnishings are displayed. Again, in earlier days, these furnishings would either have been outside, or would not have been present at all (such as the library). $15–$20

"Pierre Lafluer's Gypsy Caravan"

(On reverse side) Unused reproduction tourist postcard, color photo, by Benedikt Verlag, unnumbered, large 6.25" x 4.25", copyright 1996. Impressively decorated interior showing a comfortable living arrangement (but still without a self-contained kitchen or bathroom). $5–$10

Oh, lovely mid-century modern furniture! "See the beautiful interiors of Prairie Schooner mobile homes . . . furniture by Kinder Mfg. Co."

(On reverse side) Used advertising postcard, color photo, by H. S. Crocker, unnumbered, 5.5" x 3.5", posted 1958 from Elkhart, Indiana, to Laconia, New Hampshire. Pictured is a "Janet Lee" chair, which according to the text was part of the smart and attractive design of these mobile homes. $10–$15

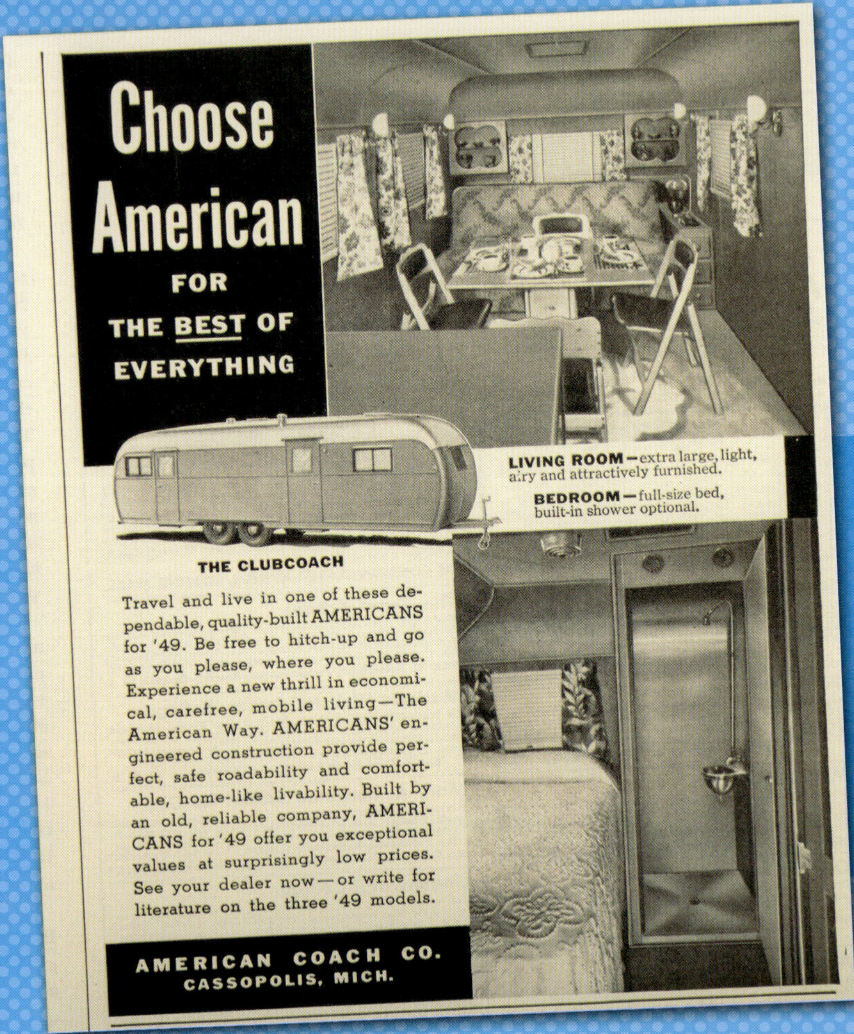

"Choose American For the Best of Everything . . . American Coach Co., Cassopolis, Mich."

Magazine advertisement, black-and-white photos, 5" x 6.25", dated 1949. Yahoo! This early ad noted the availability of "built-in shower optional" for the bedroom, at a time when self-contained bathrooms for mobile homes and travel trailers were quite a new development. Also, the coach's living room was described as "extra large, light, airy and attractively furnished." $5–$10

"Milburn Trailer Sales . . . High Quality–Low Price . . . Norfolk, Virginia"

Rare find! Drive-in theatre advertising card (with the coming movie schedule printed on the reverse side), 7.5" x 5.25", dated 1955. Highly detailed cut-away view of a huge 45-foot-long "Rocket" mobile home, showing its two bedrooms, full bathroom, kitchen, and living room. Note the hole punched on the right side of the card, so that these cards could be hung on a hook or nail at the box office for easy distribution. $15–$20

THE SATURDAY EVENING POST 91

Builders of giant B-47s happy in MOBILE HOMES!

For example, Mr. and Mrs. CHARLES BEYER, *employed at Wichita (Kan.) Division of Boeing Airplane Company*

The Beyers live in beautifully landscaped Meadowlark Trailer Park, many of whose residents work in Wichita's aircraft plants.

At Meadowlark, all water, electricity and sewer lines run underground. Two utility buildings provide automatic washers and driers; modern toilets and showers. There's a fully-equipped children's playground . . . and a full-time park manager and custodian.

The Beyers' mobile home is parked alongside one of several picnic areas with stone fireplaces, plank tables and chairs. This park is flanked by new public and parochial schools, a fine sport center with 18-hole golf course, and an attractive "Kiddieland".

"NO HOME HUNTING, no high rentals for us," say the Beyers. "We save money when we make a payment on a trailer coach. Also, the fact that your furnishings are included in the price makes it a tremendous value. And automatic heat together with the finest insulation has kept us comfortable in every type of weather all the year 'round."

HERE THE BEYERS ENTERTAIN neighbors at a steak fry. Mobile living for Charles and Lucille also includes owning both their own airplane and automobile. "We like the independence of owning our home," says he. And she adds, "Young folks often aren't permanently settled and here's a home they can take wherever their career sends them."

Priced from $2000 to $6000

including furnishings, these new TCMA trailer coaches offer attractive, mobile and moderately-priced housing for families of aircraft and other defense plant workers, construction men in the field, members of the Armed Forces, young marrieds and retired couples. Make the TCMA emblem your guide to quality and satisfaction, for the members of TCMA are the *leaders of the industry*, pioneering improved designs, building dependably to high standards.

"YOU HAVE MORE PRIVACY," says Lucille. "The bedrooms close off. Our shower is separate from the rest of our modern bathroom." And her husband, Charles, volunteers, "There's no landlord supervision, there are no neighbor problems."

"EVERYTHING'S MORE MODERN and handier in our mobile home," say the Beyers, "than in other types of housing we've seen. Fixtures and appliances are of newer design. We like the arrangement of space and facilities better. And there are plenty of cupboards and closets."

TCMA Trailer Coach Manufacturers Assn.

FREE NEW BOOK! Just out! Complete information on newest TCMA mobile homes. Write TCMA, Dept. P-32, Civic Opera Bldg., Chicago 6, Ill.

"Builders of Giant B-47s Happy in Mobile Homes!"

Magazine advertisement, black-and-white photos, four view, 10.25" x 13.5", in *Saturday Evening Post*, March 22, 1952, page 91. This large-scale ad allowed three interior views to be included—of the bedroom, living room, and kitchen of the coach. No bathroom was shown as yet. $5–$10

"Del Buckles–The Leadership Dealership . . . Phoenix"

(On reverse side) Scarce card! Unused advertising postcard, color photo, by Kolor View Press and Petley Studios, unnumbered, 5.5" x 3.5", c. 1960s–1970s. Here was the glowing description printed on the card's back: "Partial living room shines with regal readiness, one of many highlights of modern mobile home life on display at Del Buckles." $10–$15

"Americana Mobile Homes, Inc. . . . Berwick, Pa."

(On reverse side) Unused advertising postcard, color photo, no maker identified, unnumbered, 5.25" x 4", c. 1970s. Unusual card showing the floral pattern fabric of the times. The text on the reverse side noted that this card pictured a "typical living room of . . . the Berwick Series." $10–$15

"Your Furnishings Are Included In The Price Of A Mobile Home . . . Mobile Home Manufacturers Assn."

Magazine advertisement, black-and-white photo, 10.25" x 14", dated 1958. By this date, the technology had greatly advanced, as the ad emphasized, allowing for a mobile home (which might "measure 10' x 40' or more") to include a "new refrigerator, disposal, washer and dryer . . . complete bathroom with tub and shower . . . air-conditioning, built-in television if you like." $5–$10

"You're Completely 'At Home' The First Day! . . . The Mobile Home . . . Mobile Home Manufacturers Assn."

Magazine advertisement, black-and-white photo, 10.25" x 13.5", dated 1959. The detailed text of this ad read much like that of the adjacent advertisement, and it noted "many mobile homes measure 10' x 50' or more." They keep getting bigger and bigger. $5–$10

"Caerlwan Caravan Parks, Talybont, Inside One Holiday Caravan."

Scarce piece! Used advertising postcard, black-and-white photo, by Judges' Ltd., 5.5" x 3.5", posted 1965 from Merioneth to Bucks, England. The handwritten message on the back: "On the card is a picture of our caravan. It's a very roomy, nice one, and we have a double bed." We do not know whether this coach would have been a holiday rental unit, or whether the senders would have purchased it. $15–$20

"Is YOUR Bathroom This Modern? . . . Mobile Home Manufacturers Assn."

Magazine advertisement, black-and-white photo, 10.25" x 13.5", in *Life* magazine, c. late 1950s. What a roomy bath! $5–$10

"The Geer Company . . . Grand Island, Nebraska"

(On reverse side) Unused advertising postcard, color photo, by Rollie Studio, #48809, 5.5" x 3.5", c. 1960s. Printed on back side: "A typical example of the custom built interiors available in Geer Mobile Homes." It did look elegant, even sporting a fireplace! See the adjacent card as well. $10–$15

Hallelujah for self-contained bathrooms! "We Chose A Mobile Home For Complete, Modern Comfort . . . Trailer Coach Manufacturers Assn."

Magazine advertisement, black-and-white photos, five view, 9.75" x 13", in *Saturday Evening Post*, September 26, 1953, page 100. Finally, mobile-home bathrooms came out of the closet and could be pictured in advertising. See the next ad as well. $5–$10

"Geer Mobile Homes . . . Grand Island, Nebr."

(On reverse side) Unused advertising postcard, color photo, by Bailey Studio, #19834, 5.5" x 3.5", c. 1950s–1960s. The text: "This beautiful Youngstown kitchen with Automatic washer, Deluxe Range and large 11 cubic foot refrigerator is standard (not optional) in all 46 foot and 51 foot Geer Mobile Homes." Kitchens sell coaches. $5–$10

"Geer Mobile Homes, Grand Island, Nebraska"

(On reverse side) Unused advertising postcard, color photo, by Bailey Studio, #1162B, 5.5" x 3.5", c. 1960s. Look what the short text printed on the reverse side stated: "Gracious living is yours in this luxurious 51-foot 10-foot wide Geer mobile Home." Wow! It was big and fancy. $10–$15

Remarkable Rare find!

Lengthy caption/text on front: "Now Zimmer Diagonal Design brings you a new concept of living comfort. See it today in this 33-ft. 'Salon' model. You can enjoy a new way of life now! Own a Zimmer Trailer Home." Used advertising postcard, black-and-white photo, by Meteor Photo Company, unnumbered, 5.5" x 3.5", posted 1950 from/to Springfield, Massachusetts. This striking picture certainly made the coach look modern at the time. $30–$40

"There's New Dimension In Mobile Home Living."

Magazine advertisement, black-and-white photo, 10.25" x 13.25", dated 1963. The text pointed out that "the average cost is about $5500" for a new mobile home. "New mobile homes have one to four bedrooms. One or two baths. Sizes to 10' x 65'—some models are 12' wide, others expand to 16'–20' wide." Wow! That could be 1,000–1,200 square feet! $5–$10

"Early American by Schult . . . Famous For Quality"

(On reverse side) Unique card! Advertising postcard, color photo, by Dexter Color Illinois, #1621-C, 5.5" x 3.5", c. 1960s. This unusual card was printed with a fill-in-the-blanks format to thank prospective customers for visiting Schult. In part, the text read: "We enjoyed showing you around and hope you saw a mobile home you liked." $10–$15

"Ankney Trailer Sales . . . Orlando, Fla."

Rare find! Used advertising postcard, linen, by Douglas Smith, 5.5" x 3.5", unnumbered, posted 1957 from Orlando, Florida, to Barberton, Ohio. The text on the reverse side referred to "Ankney Mobile Home Sales" and to the availability of both "New and Used Mobile Homes." This wonderful card also illustrated a cut-away view of a one bedroom coach, which included its bathroom and kitchen-living area. $15–$20

"A new television is placed in a mobile home, 1954."

(On reverse side) Unused reproduction postcard, black-and-white photo, by Corbis–Bettmann and Abbeville Publishing, unnumbered, over-sized 6.5" x 4.75", dated 1999. It was a very important development when mobile homes were equipped with such a highly popular technological advancement as televisions. It helped put them on par with stick-built homes. $10–$15

"Prairie Schooner (Elkhart, Indiana . . . Elkton, Maryland)"

Fun, fun, fun! Unused advertising postcard, color photo, no maker identified, unnumbered, 3.5" x 5.5", c. 1950s. This clever card showed only a portion of the 33.5-foot-long "Century Limited" mobile home model. The creative porch and awning was a unique feature for a mobile home at the time. The text on the card explained: "New kind of mobile home. Now you can greet your family and friends at the front door! They don't have to climb in from the side as with ordinary trailers." It brought the outdoors right up to the coach's front door. $20–$25

"The famous Urban Aluminum Awning, as featured nationally on the popular television program Maverick."

(On reverse side) "Urban Industries . . . Galion, Ohio . . . Azusa, California." Unused advertising postcard, color photo, by McCoy Color Studios and Dexter Press, #35964-B, 5.5" x 3.5", c. 1950s. Picture perfect! A spacious awning-covered outside area increased the usable living space of a mobile home dramatically—especially in warm weather. $10–$15

"Mobile Home Accessories . . . Aluminum Patio Covers . . . Custom Porches and Steps . . . Imperial Metal Products . . . Huntington Beach, California"

(On reverse side) Rare find! Unused advertising postcard, color photo, by Dexter Press, #19518-C, 5.5" x 3.5", c. 1960s–1970s. This unique card contained a fill-in-the-blanks area for a mobile-home owner to contact the company "for a free estimate without obligation." $10–$15

Chapter 8

Location, Location, Location

In this chapter, we will explore two distinct aspects about the location of some mobile homes—two matters about which many people may have never thought. First, quite a number of amateur radio operators have lived in mobile homes. And, when it comes to radio connections, location is a primary element affecting the sending and receipt of radio calls. In earlier decades (especially until about the 1970s), many amateur radio enthusiasts prepared and exchanged QSL cards (cards confirming successful reception of a radio signal) or postcards between one another to document and record in writing their radio connections. Some of those radio operators created personalized QSL cards with graphics showing features about themselves, such as their mobile homes, for those individuals who resided in house trailers. Several samples are included here.

The second location issue covered here involves the many mobile homes situated in foreign countries, because house trailers have been very popular outside as well as in the USA. Of course, in order for another country to be home to house trailers, the country must have a suitable economy, climate, and terrain to foster this form of housing. Many advanced industrial nations qualify, and we have included examples in this chapter showing some of their impressive mobile homes, often called caravans and caravan parks.

"Scenic Overlook"
(On reverse side) Unused art postcard, from a painting by Paige Bridges, 5.5" x 4.25", c. 2000s. This mobile home image has always reminded us of the fabulously funny mountain driving sequence from the classic Lucy-Desi movie *The Long, Long Trailer*. $10–$15

"Everything Is O.K. . . . Camping Here For The Night."

Three comic advertising postcards, one used, two unused, by Laff Gram, #R-50, 5.5" x 3.5", c. 1960s (one posted 1969). Laff Gram very successfully sold many varieties of fun card graphics, and often sold the same scenes to multiple businesses—as was the case here. Great exaggeration! How could the small car tow the lengthy six-wheel house trailer, and don't forget the boat—straight up?! When some people conjure up images of trailer trash, this is the kind of scene they imagine. $5–$10

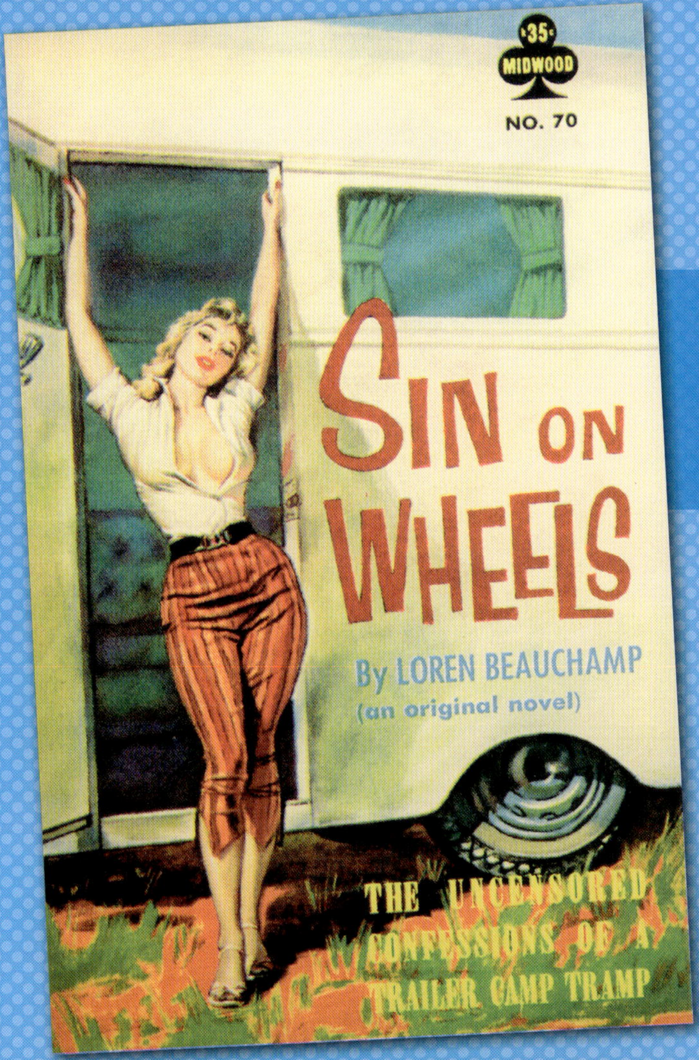

"Sin On Wheels . . . The Uncensored Confessions Of A Trailer Camp Tramp . . . By Loren Beauchamp (an original novel)."

(On reverse side) Great title! Unused advertising postcard, by Pulp Postcards and Prion Books (London), #70, 5" x 6.75", c. 2000s. $5–$10

"Your Trailer Park Called . . . Their Trash Is Missing."

Unused comic postcard, by Live Out Loud, unnumbered, 6" x 4", c. 2010s. Too cute! $5–$10

Unique wood coach find! "We've moved!"

Unused wooden postcard, by Liz Young and Spitfire Girl, unnumbered, 6" x 4", c. 2000s. On the reverse side of this unusual modern card depicting a vintage mobile home is a fill-in-the-blank format for the sender to provide her/his new address and phone information. $10–$15

Call letters: "W7YFL."

Used QSL postcard, 5.5" x 3.5", posted 1957 from/to Portland, Oregon. Notice that this and several other radio cards shown in the chapter referred to the trailer park where the sender resided—in this case in the "Tall Firs Trailer Park." And, a long and detailed image of a 1950s era mobile home (of course, with an attached radio antenna) was displayed in the card's lower left quadrant. $10–$15

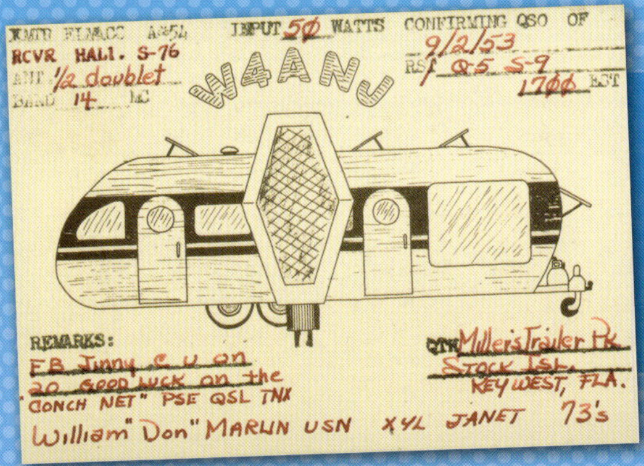

Call letters: "W4ANJ."

Used QSL postcard, 5.5" x 3.5", posted 1953 from Key West, Florida, to Haverhill, Massachusetts. Spectacular graphic of a handsome mobile home with a large radio microphone in the foreground! The amateur radio station was in Miller's Trailer Park, on Stock Island, Key West. $20–$25

Great amateur radio humor! Call letters "KFA-8110 . . . I told you it was too heavy."

Unused QSL card, 5.5" x 3.5", from Nipomo, California, c. 1960s. Some of the tall radio antennas on the roofs of mobile homes must cause people to wonder. $10–$15

"Portable Mobile W6SRT"

Used QSL postcard, 5.5" x 3.5", posted in 1947 from San Francisco, California, to Tarrytown, New York. This delightful humorous card illustrated a struggling tow vehicle pulling a house on wheels, complete with its radio antenna and outhouse also on wheels. $15–$20

Call letters: KID8939.

(Above) Used (but not mailed) QSL card, 5.5" x 3.5", Waynesboro, Pennsylvania, c. 1960s–1970s. Two of the brightest QSL cards we have seen! $5–$10

Call letters: KBA9566

(Below) Unused QSL card, 5.5" x 3.5", Easthampton, Massachusetts, c. 1960s–1970s. Wonderful hand-drawn mobile home, complete with roof-top radio antennae! $5–$10

Call letters"KFD 2400. The Voice of the Trailer Industry"

Used (but not posted) QSL mobile-home advertising postcard, color photo, 5.5" x 3.5", dated 1964 from Benicia, California. Unique generic card printed on the reverse side with a fill-in-the-blank form for amateur radio operators, and printed with an advertisement for "the magnificent new Fleetwood Broadmore Custom . . . outstanding example of modern mobile home engineering." The sale's pitch also touted "Fleetwood's timeless beauty and lasting value ..." $10–$15

Unusual find! Call letters: KMX1583. "San Luis Rey 'Own Your Own' Mobile Estates"

(On reverse side) Unused advertising QSL postcard, color photo, 5.5" x 3.5", Oceanside, California, c. 1970s. This novel QSL card is an advertisement for an upscale mobile home park, as pictured—showing a handsome recreation hall and well-dressed couple playing croquet on the manicured lawn. $10–$15

Call letters: "KBA1968"

(Above) Used (but not mailed) advertising QSL card, 5.5" x 3.5", Chester, Illinois, c. 1960s–1970s. The attractive graphic on the card was a stock image adopted by this dealership. $5–$10

Call letters: KLK0053. "Lincoln Mobile Homes, Inc."

(Below) Used QSL postcard, black and white, referencing "S.S.S. Mobile Homes," 5.5" x 3.5", posted 1962 from Templeton to Montgomery, Massachusetts. The unusual black background for this detailed hand-drawn card resulted in a dramatic image of its impressive mobile home. $10–$15

Call letters: KNN6524

Unused QSL card, 5.5" x 3.5", Grand Rapids, Michigan, c. 1960s–1970s. Impressive and stylish raised-roof coach! $5–$10

Call letters: KPC3884

(Above) Used (but not mailed) QSL card, by Calypso QSL Cards, 5.5" x 3.5", Banks, Oregon, dated 1960s (printed "196_" on back). Although many QSL cards were home-made by individual radio operators, this card was professionally made—as were many others. The graphic showed a long mobile home with sliding glass doors and a roof-top radio antennae. $5–$10

Call letters: KEB3769. Handle: "Always Mobile"

(Below) Used (but not mailed) QSL card, 5.5" x 3.5", Tulsa, Oklahoma, c. 1960s. Notice that the radio antennae depicted here was on the tow car's bumper, rather than on the coach's roof. Incidentally, the car and mobile home were not shown in proper proportions, and this automobile should not have attempted to pull such a large coach. $5–$10

Call letters: K4CRF

Used QSL advertising postcard, black-and-white photo, 5.5" x 3.5", "Wertz Mobile Homes Inc.," posted 1976 from Orangeburg, South Carolina, to Phoenix, Arizona. Numerous dealers used amateur radio and QSL cards to promote their mobile home businesses. $10–$15

Call letters: KPC1767

Unused QSL card, 5.5" x 3.5", Lexington, Washington, c. 1960s–1970s. Clever text: "If you can't drag it—Park it at TIM-WA Trailer Estates." $5–$10

Call letters: KHA-8285

Used QSL postcard, black and white, 5.5" x 3.5", Grayville, Illinois, posted 1963 to Lititz, Pennsylvania. Note that the long, hand-drawn mobile home has a slide-out entrance room. $5–$10

Call letters: KNE-1091

Bright graphics! Unused QSL card, 5.5" x 3.5", Chetenne, Wyoming, c. 1960s–1970s. Notice that the mobile home has been named "Rollahome." We like the dog! $5–$10

Call letters: KID8939

Unused QSL card, 5.5" x 3.5", Waynesboro, Pennsylvania, c. 1960s–1970s. Another impressive raised-roof coach. $5–$10

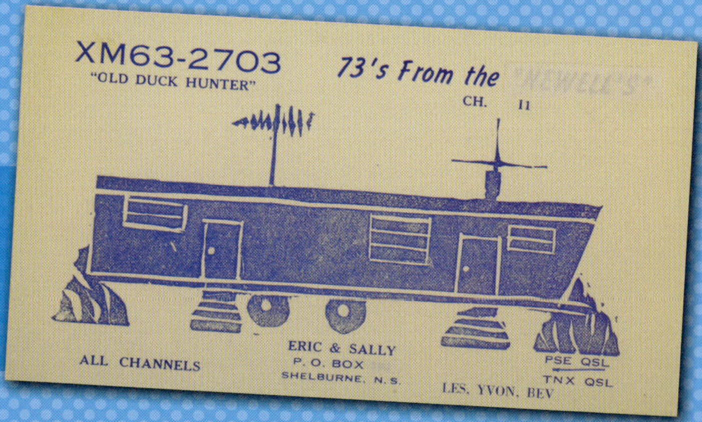

Call letters: XM63-2703

Unused QSL card, 5.5" x 3", Shelburne, Nova Scotia, Canada, c. 1960s–1970s. Handsome, big mobile home, with radio antennae. $5–$10

Call letters: W4RDF

Used (but not mailed) QSL card, 5.5" x 3.5", Norfolk, Virginia, dated 1950. A long and stylish house trailer! $10–$15

Call letters: KCM0268

Used (but not mailed) QSL card, 5.5" x 3.5", Santa Fe Trailer Court, Olathe, Kansas, c. 1960s–1970s. Showing a long, upscale mobile home. This is one of only a few vintage QSL cards we have found that was created for a female radio operator. $5–$10

Call letters: KPM0705

Used (but not mailed) QSL card, 5.5" x 3.5", Mt. Morris, Michigan, dated 1966. Notice the large hand-drawn mobile home, with a radio antennae on the front portion of the roof. $5–$10

Call letters: KRD3971

Unused QSL card, 5.5" x 3.5", Torrance, California, c. 1960s–1970s. This card shows a sizable house trailer being towed by a pick-up truck, with the radio antennae on the roof of the truck. $5–$10

Call letters: KHJ4892

Used (but not mailed) QSL card, 5.5" x 3.5", Columbus, Ohio, c. 1960s–1970s. Impressive mobile home, with a tall roof antennae. $5–$10

"The Orchards Caravan and Camping Park, Newbridge" (Isle of Wight)

(On reverse side) Unused advertising postcard, color photo, by Nigh and Sons, #KIW814, 5.5" x 3.5", c. 1970s–1980s. Simple, but stylish, British mobile homes. $5–$10

"Dan's Mobile Homes and Parks Ltd . . . Ottawa, Ontario, Canada."

(On reverse side) Unused advertising postcard, color aerial photo, by Newton Photographic, #C-1634, 3.5" x 5.5", c. 1970s–1980s. The text on the card's back noted: "Modern hook-ups for mobile homes. . . . New and used mobile homes for sale." $5–$10

"Fallbarrow Caravan Park, Windermere, English Lake District"

(On reverse side) Unused advertising postcard, color photo, by Sanderson and Dixon and Colourpicture (USA), #SD670 and #P62197, 5.5" x 3.5", c. 1960s–1970s. What a charming water-view location for these mobile homes. $5–$10

"Camping Lede En Oudewaard" (Netherlands)

(Above) (On reverse side) Used advertising postcard, black-and-white photo, by Hartogh, #776, 5.5" x 3.5", c. 1960s–1970s (postmark illegible). This vintage card showed several sizable caravans permanently situated in the park. $5–$10

"Fell End Caravan Park, Hale, Beetham, Westmorland" (England)

(Below) (On reverse side) Unused advertising postcard, color photo, by Jarrold and Sons and Sanderson and Dixon, #KLD379, c. 1960s–1970s. It was clear that the large caravans in this upscale park were permanently situated. $5–$10

"The Doonpark Caravan Site located on Scotland's Solway Firth"

(Above) Used advertising postcard, color photo, by Hail Caledonia and Whiteholme Publishers, #5211, 5.75" x 4", posted 1978 from Scotland to England (postmark/address partially illegible). $5–$10

"Lydstep Haven" (England)

(Below) Used (but not mailed) advertising postcard, color photo, by Archway Publicity (Wales), #P97, 6" x 4", c. 1970s–80s. Magnificent water views! $5–$10

"Orchard Caravan Park, Bognor Regis, West Sussex" (England)

(Above) Used advertising postcard, color photo, by Bennett Publications, #7823, 6" x 4", posted 1981 from West Sussex to Kent, England. The grounds of a former orchard would made a lovely spot for a mobile home park. $5–$10

"Britain In Bloom, Prizewinning Mobile Home Park"

(Below) (On reverse side) Unused advertising postcard, color photo, by Jerome Dessain and Co., #C24599, 5.5" x 3.5", c. 1970s. Picture perfect! $5–$10

"Old Mill Caravan Park . . . St. Helens, Isle of Wight" (England)

(Above) (On reverse side) Unused advertising postcard, color photo, by Chudley and Son, c. 1960s–1970s. What a marvelous arrangement that the mobile homes away from the water were elevated to maximize their views of the waterway. $5–$10

"Sarnfaen Caravan Park, Talybont, Gwynedd" (England)

(Below) Unused advertising postcard, color photo, by Judges Limited, #C3864X, 6" x 4", c. 1970s–1980s. These large caravans (mobile homes) enjoyed lovely views of the countryside. As is the case the world over, proximity to the water is valued for mobile home locations. $5–$10

"Part of Downton Camp" (England)

(On reverse side) Used (but not mailed) tourist postcard, chrome, no maker identified, unnumbered, 6" x 4", dated 1959 (handwritten note). At the time, these smaller caravans were about the largest house trailers available. $5–$10

"A Corner of Rosneath Castle Caravan Park" (Scotland)

Used advertising postcard, color photo, no maker identified, #PAT875, 5.5" x 3.5" with scalloped edges, posted 1939 from Glasgow, Scotland, to Norfolk, England. Throughout Europe, the grounds of numerous castles were used as caravan parks to help support the estates. Another attractive setting! $10–$15

"Maddieson's Caravan Park . . . Sussex" (England)

(On reverse side) Used advertising postcard, color photo, by Colourpicture (USA), #WB676, 5.5" x 3.5", posted 1968 from Kent to Bucks, England. A relaxed scene, complete with a flower garden. According to the text, this park rented "4–6 berth caravans." $5–$10

Chapter 9

Heaven on Wheels

We have heard of lots of mobile homes and mobile-home parks being described as "heavenly" or "heaven on earth"—which suggests to us that the view of them from above must be particularly inspiring. But there is a problem. How can mobiles be heavenly? They cannot fly, and they cannot even leave the ground. Or, maybe mobile homes *can* sometimes get off the ground?

In any event, we decided to put our basic thinking to the test and to assemble a group of aerial views of mobile homes and their resting places. We discovered a treasure trove of aerial images because such pictures have been very popular among advertisers over the years. Aerial shots tell a lot that we cannot see from the ground. They illustrate the size and scope of mobile-home locations (including amenities like swimming pools, shuffleboard courts, and recreation halls), and they show the surrounding areas and their attributes (such as highways, waterways, and shopping centers). To put it simply, aerial pictures are impressive! So, this chapter is our look from above, or "heaven on wheels."

How'd they do that?! High-rise mobile home tenement?!
Color photo, no maker identified, unnumbered, 10" x 8", c. 1970s–1980s. And, why would anyone do this? $10–$15

Too cute! Title "Vintage Roswell"
(On reverse side) Unused art postcard, from a painting by artist Paige Bridges, 5.5" x 4.25", c. 2010s. $5–$10

Fun, fun, fun! "USCG AIRFAC Muskegon . . . 'trailer trash' . . . 'Naturalus Selectus Interuptus!'"
Fabric patch, 5" in diameter, c. 1990s–2000s. Notice that this colorful and humorous patch showed both a recliner chair with wings attached to it and a mobile home or house trailer complete with roof-mounted TV dish and pink flamingo yard ornament. $5–$10

"God Bless Our Trailer Home."
Decorative ceramic plate, made in Japan, by Kelvin, #X-424, 8" round (with six scalloped-edge sections), c. 1950s–1960s. Scarce piece! This fabulous find featuring a lavender house trailer was manufactured with two holes in its rim on the back of the plate along with a wire hanger, so that it could readily be hung on display in the proud owner's mobile home. $10–$15

"Slice of Heaven" and "Double High"
Board game cards, 3.5" x 2.25", from Trailer Park Wars game, copyright 2007. Some mobile homes are located so that they can sit atop basement foundations, or atop first-floor walls/garages/carports. For the boxed game, $20–$25

Up, up, and away!

Press photo, architectural rendering, black and white, no maker identified, unnumbered, 10" x 8", dated 1970. The newspaper story about this nine-unit, three-story design noted it was to be called SkyRise and was proposed to be built in St. Paul, Minnesota. As the article quipped, the design certainly would have taken "mobile" out of "mobile home." $10–$15

Heaven, or hell, on wheels?! "Department 56 . . . Snow Village Halloween . . . Lot 13, Crystal Lake"

Ceramic mobile home decorative model, with working lights, in original box, measuring 10.5" x 6.5" x 6.5", copyright 2011. This piece is pure, unadulterated trailer trash! Note the items out in front of the coach—the antiquated refrigerator, the stately wingback chair, and the ever-ready shotgun. A pair of legs and feet are even shown sticking out from underneath the porch. Are they real, or just a spooky hoax? $100-$125

It's like a fairy tale–owning a tiny, tiny trailer house. "It's within your realm. . . . Venture. The little castle on wheels."

Magazine advertisement, by Starcraft Company, 8" x 10.75", dated 1975. This fun and very clever advertising attempted to make the pop-up camper look spacious, but we are not so sure whether this type of publicity might have backfired and might have served only to remind people of how cramped all trailers and mobile homes are when compared to castles and even standard homes. Since there are no size restrictions to distinguish travel trailers from mobile homes or house trailers, even this tiny castle could be a mobile home, and we have seen people residing in pop-up coaches for quite extended periods of time. $5–$10

"Hollywood Trailer Park . . . St. Petersburg, Florida"

(On reverse side) Unused advertising postcard, color aerial photo, by Dexter Press, #75925-B, 3.5" x 5.5", c. 1950s. The text printed on the card's back boasted: "Lots for the largest mobile homes." $5–$10

"Newport Harbor, California"

(On reverse side) Used tourist postcard, color aerial photo, by George Watson and H. S. Crocker, unnumbered, 5.5" x 3.5", posted 1961 from Newport Beach, California, to Poland Spring, Maine. This photo, dated 1957, showed a mobile-home dealership along the highway. $5–$10

"The Anchorage Mobile Homes Park . . . Delray Beach, Florida"

(On reverse side) Used advertising postcard, color aerial photo, by Sheets Photography and Dexter Press, #22463-C, 5.5" x 3.5", posted 1972 from Delray Beach, Florida, to Phoenix, Arizona. This aerial image revealed an attractive mobile home location on the intra-coastal waterway. $5–$10

Water, water, everywhere! "Yacht Haven Mobile Home Park . . . Fort Lauderdale, Florida"

(Above) Unused advertising postcard, color aerial photo, by Smith Aerial Surveys and Dukane Press, #8234, 5.5" x 3.5", c. 1960s–1970s. This card's text spoke of "waterfront vistas." It also noted: "Situated on the South Fork of the New River in Ft. Lauderdale, this fine park offers a picturesque setting for Mobile Homes . . . Most mobile home sites feature private docks for yachts." Very high-end. $5–$10

"Gulf Stream Trailer Park and Marina" (Marathon, Florida Keys)

(Below) Unused advertising postcard, color aerial view, by Colourpicture, #P69092, 5.5" x 3.5", c. 1960s. These mobile homes were situated in an ideal location, according to the card's text, having the "Nation's Finest Fishing And Climate." $5–$10

"Windmill Village . . . World's Most Picturesque Mobile Home Park . . . North Fort Myers, Florida"

(Above) (On reverse side) Unused advertising postcard, color aerial photo, by Punta Gorda Postcard, #32633, 5.5" x 3.5", c. 1960s–1970s. This large facility had 500 mobile home lots, each with a minimum size of 50' x 75 '. $5–$10

"Johnson's Mobile Home Park, West Memphis, Arkansas"

(Below) Unused advertising card, color aerial photo, no maker identified, unnumbered, 5.5" x 3.5", c. 1960s. $5–$10

A heavenly photo op! "The Beautiful Pla-Mor Mobile Village nestled in the valley at the foot of Pikes Peak in Colorado Springs, Colorado"

(On reverse side) Unused advertising postcard (with fold mark), black-and-white aerial photo, no maker identified, unnumbered, large 8.75" x 6", c. 1950s. This park was built with room for additional mobile homes to be sited there. Rare big card. $15–$20

Just One Mobile Home

Unused tourist postcard, black-and-white aerial photo, no maker identified, unnumbered, 5.5" x 3.5", c. 1950s–1960s. This scene illustrated one of the popular uses of mobile homes—as housing on or near large farms where extended farm families or farmhands could live close to their workplaces. $10–$15

"City Mobile Homes Park Ltd. . . . Vimont, Laval" (Quebec, Canada)

(Above) Unused advertising postcard, black-and-white aerial photo, no maker identified, unnumbered, 5.25" x 3.5", c. 1950s–1960s. We have seen many examples in this book of the international popularity of mobile home living. $10–$15

"Trailer Camp at Riverdale" (North Dakota)

(Below) Used advertising postcard, black-and-white aerial photo, by Aerial Photo Service and Saks News Agency, unnumbered, 5.5" x 3.5", posted 1955 from Minot, North Dakota, to Lincoln, Nebraska. Interestingly, almost all of the house trailers neatly lined up at this facility appeared to be identical—same size, same design. They were probably permanently set up on their sites, and then rented or sold. The senders of the card were living at this park and mentioned in their handwritten message that they were going to the Friday-night dance in Minot. $10–$15

Fields of mobiles! "Mesa Mobile Home Parks" (Phoenix, Arizona)

Unused advertising postcard, color aerial photo, by Petley Studios, #X116988, 6" x 4", c. 1980s. According to the text: "Typical of the vast complexes of mobile homes East of Mesa accommodating winter visitors in the valley of the sun." $5–$10

Lovely lake side location. "Cordova Mobile Home Park . . . On Beautiful Lake Cranbury . . . Cranbury, Texas"

(On reverse side) Unused advertising postcard, color aerial photo, by David Malone, #119895, 5.5" x 3.5", c. 1960s. $5–$10

"LaJoie's Grocery And Trailer Park" (near Soo, Michigan)

(Above) Unused advertising postcard, black-and-white aerial photo, by L. L. Cook Co., unnumbered, 5.5" x 3.5", c. 1950s. This small park was populated by some very large mobile homes. $5–$10

Large mobile home location

(Below) Used tourist postcard, black-and-white aerial photo, no maker identified, unnumbered, 5.5" x 3.5", posted 1959 from Eau Gallie, Florida, to Vineland, New Jersey. In earlier years, many mobile home facilities were situated in more isolated areas. It would be interesting to see how this park's surroundings look today. $5–$10

"Pot-Nets Park . . . Luxurious Mobile Home Living . . . Indian River Bay . . . Sussex County, Delaware"

(On reverse side) Unused advertising postcard, color aerial photo, by Thurston Studio and Dexter Press, #67220-C, 5.5" x 3.5", c. 1960s. What great water views and water access! $5–$10

"Paradise Palms Trailer Park" (Mesa, Arizona)

(On reverse side) Used advertising postcard, linen, three-view, by Ad-Craft Line, #19,543F, 5.5" x 3.5", posted 1959 from Mesa, Arizona, to Billings, Montana. Try repeating this park's slogan rapidly ten times: "Particular People Prefer Paradise Palms Park." $5–$10

"High Point Mobile Home Park and Sales . . . Enid, Oklahoma"

Unused advertising postcard, black-and-white aerial photo, no maker identified, unnumbered, 5.5" x 3.5", c. 1960s. What an efficient and geometrical design of this park. $5–$10

"Gasparilla Mobile Estates, Placida, Florida"

(On reverse side) Unused advertising postcard, color aerial photo, by Harris Photography and Dexter Press, #55894-D, 5.5" x 3.5", c. 1960s–1970s. Though somewhat difficult to see in this picture, many of these mobile homes were on canals with water access to the Gulf of Mexico. $5–$10

Unique card! "Lydstep Haven" (Wales)

This card advertised a visitors guidebook, rather than a caravan park. Unused advertising postcard, color aerial photo, by Alan Shepherd (author) Publishing, #CVLY6, 5.75" x 4", c. 1980s. What a truly picturesque setting for these mobile homes! $5–$10

"St. Tudwal's Bay, Abersoch"

(On reverse side) Used advertising postcard, color aerial photo, no maker identified, #PT24125, 5.5" x 3.5", posted 1970 from Caernarvonshire to Plymouth, England. The lucky folks who sent this card were staying in a caravan right down by the beach and the water. $5–$10

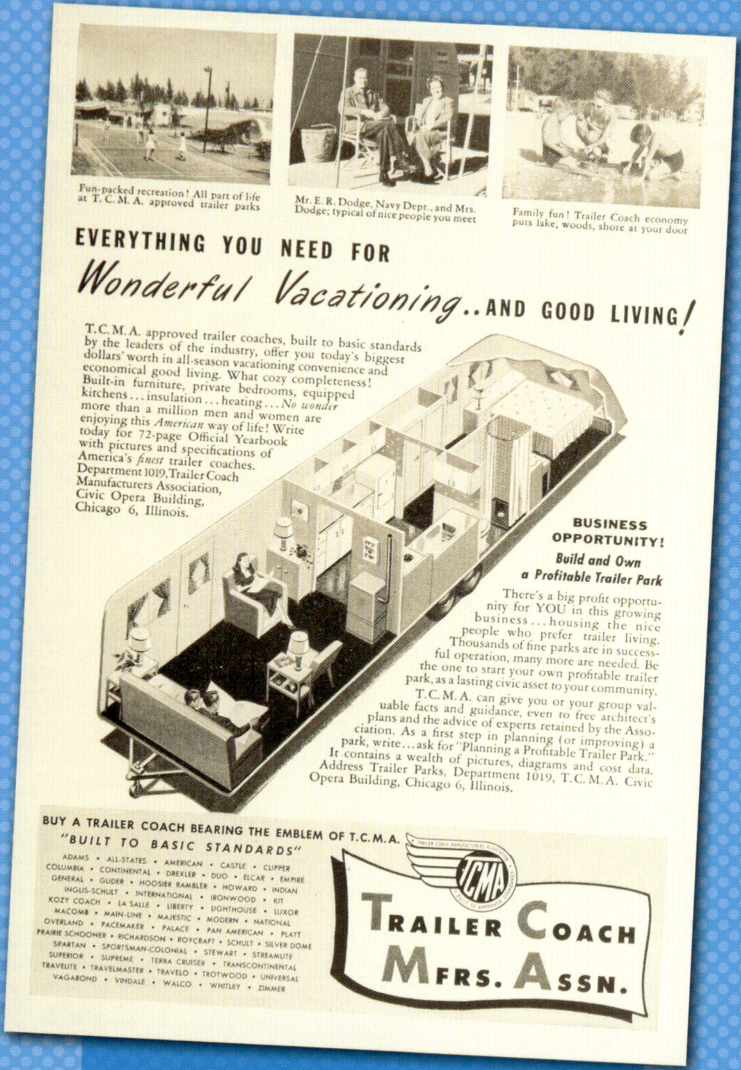

"Everything You Need For Wonderful Vacationing . . . And Good Living!"

Magazine advertisement, black and white, four-view, with aerial cutaway graphic, 6.5" x 10", c. late 1940s–1950s. The sizable house trailer would have to have been at least thirty to thirty-five feet in length. $5–$10

"Cloch Caravans, Gourock" (Great Britain)

Used advertising postcard, color photo, by Photo Precision, #RB30, 5.5" x 3.5", posted 1968 from Gourock (address partially illegible). What a comfortable country setting this park appeared to be. $5–$10

"Portland Mobile Home Court" (Portland, Oregon)

Unused advertising postcard, color aerial photo, by Techniphoto and Action Color, #52132, 5.5" x 3.5", c. 1960s–1970s. $5–$10

A personal favorite card of ours–with such balanced composition and handsome earth-tone colors. "St. Andrews and the East Sands from Kinkell Braes" (Scotland)

(On reverse side) Used tourist postcard, color aerial photo, by Whyte Publishing, #DJ19, 6" x 4", posted 1990 to Suffolk, England (postmark partially illegible). $10–$15

"Brown's Cliff Farm Caravan Park, Cayton Bay, Nr. Scarborough"

(Above) Unused advertising postcard, two-view, color aerial photos, by Dennis and Sons Ltd., #12, 6" x 4", c. 1970s–1980s. The large caravan at the right side of this card looks so much like an American mobile home. $5–$10

"New Quay" (England)

(Below) Used tourist postcard, color aerial photo, by Dennis and Sons Ltd., #N.2606, 5.5" x 3.5", posted 1983 from Llandysul to Lancs, England. The senders of this card, who were staying at this caravan park, not surprisingly, wrote that we "think it's great" here. $5–$10

"Freshwater Caravan Park, Burton Bradstock" (England)

(On reverse side) Used advertising postcard, color aerial photo, by Photo Precision Limited, #R4651, 5.5" x 3.5", posted 1977 from Dorchester to Southampton, England. The sender, in his message, called this location a "very nice site." It certainly looked great. $5–$10

"Woodlands Holiday Park, Towyn, Merioneth" (England)

(On reverse side) Used advertising postcard, color aerial photo, by Dixon-Lotus Production, #2512, 6" x 4", posted 1975 from Aberystwyth to Derbyshire, England. The card's senders, who were staying in a caravan at this park, happily wrote: "It is a lovely site here and everywhere looks grand." $5–$10

"Haggerston Castle" (Holiday Park, Beal, Northumberland, England)

Used advertising postcard, three-view, color photos (one aerial), by Dennis and Sons Ltd., #HG/5L, 6" x 4", posted 1989 from Berwick-On-Tweed, England, to Perth, Scotland. The multi-view postcard has been particularly popular in Great Britain. See the below card as well. $5–$10

"Haggerston Castle Caravan (Park, Beal, Northumberland" England)

(On reverse side) Used advertising postcard, color aerial photo, no maker identified, unnumbered, posted 1970 to Middlesbrough, England (postmark partially illegible). As we have mentioned, many castles around the UK have become partly occupied by caravan parks to support the expenses of such formidable estates. $5–$10

Chapter 10

To Park, or Not to Park?

Ah . . . so many choices. Do we buy a small travel trailer, or a bigger stick-built house, or a mobile home? Once we get our mobile home, do we tow it around, or do we locate it somewhere more or less permanently? Where do be put it—here or there? Do we buy a parcel of land and put the mobile home there, or do we move it to a mobile-home court? What kinds of amenities and surroundings do we want close by our mobile home?

And, most importantly to us, what do we get to do in this last chapter? Well, we get to cover some worthy mobile home topics that just did not really fit into the earlier chapters and some mobile home images too good to be left out. We get to decide about the last pictures with which to leave you, as we know that last impressions can become lasting impressions. It's refreshing to find in this section several images of mobile homes in the arts of painting and photography and as the models for toys. Most certainly, such images help to debunk the trailer trash myth.

Yahoo!

Unused tourist postcard, from a color photo by Seida Bacon, unnumbered, 5.5" x 4", copyright 2010. Classic trailer trash. It's old; it's got an offensive TV dish on the roof; it's got picket fencing to serve as skirting around the perimeter of the trailer frame and tongue; it's got a roof-over of some sort; and, it's got two skinny pink flamingos in the "yard." It's got class! $5–$10

"Vintage Trailer and Matching Tractor in Dale, TX"

(On reverse side) Unused tourist postcard, color photo, by Zazzle, unnumbered, 5.5" x 4.25", c. 2010s. We wonder if this tractor had been used to pull the small house trailer, and when anyone had last lived there? $5–$10

"Home Sweet Home"

(On reverse side) Unused tourist postcard, black-and-white photo by James Soffer and Last Shot Inc., unnumbered, 6" x 4", copyright 1994. This coach could be the longest one we have ever seen—appearing to be about seventy to eighty feet in length! $5–$10

Home on the range?

(Above) Black-and-white photo, 5" x 3.5", unnumbered, dated 1964. $5–$10

"Slim's Place in the Ghost Town of Ballarat in Panamint Valley (Calif.)"

(Below) (On reverse side) Unused tourist postcard, color photo, by Chris Card and Dexter Press, #7759, 5.5" x 3.5", c. 1970s. Until his passing in 1968, this site was inhabited by one of the region's last old-time prospectors (and according to the text on the card, even he had given up the use of a burro for a Jeep). This picture proves, once again, that the size of a coach does not determine whether it can serve as a mobile home. $5–$10

Po' White Trash and the Trailer Park Symphony

Music CD, by Pocket Change Productions, copyright 2001. Featuring such mobile home owners' favorites as "Creepin'," "Cottage Cheese," and "Back It Up." Let's dance! $10–$15

"Trailercana by Antsy McClain and the Trailer Park Troubadours"

Music CD, by DPR Records, copyright 2007. Featuring such classic songs as: "Living In Aluminum," "KOA Refugee," and "Prozac Made Me Stay." Let's party! $10–$15

"Stove? Yah. I think I turned it off."

Unused comic tourist postcard, by Glenn Devery, #43, 5.5" x 3.5", copyright 1955. Fire in a moving vehicle is a serious hazard, like this example in which half the house trailer had been burned away. Rare card! $15–$20

Fire!

Color photo, 4" square, c. 1960s–1970s. Notice the snow everywhere. Probably, because of the cold, heaters were on, and something accidentally started the blaze that consumed this coach. $5–$10

"White Christmas (and) Holiday Getaway . . . By artist Paige Bridges"

(On reverse side) Unused art postcards, from paintings by Paige Bridges, unnumbered, 5" x 4.25", c. 2010s. Each, $5–$10.

"With Warmest Wishes From Our Home To Your Home." "Season's Greetings"

(On reverse side) Unused holiday postcard, by Floridian Card Products, #FPC-28, 6" x 4", c. 1970s–1980s. Notice the clever play with language—"warmest wishes" at winter time from warm-weather Florida, and "from our (mobile) home to your home." A large double-wide mobile home was depicted, with palm trees in the yard, and Santa and Mrs. Claus on the driveway. $5–$10

(On box side) "Mobile Home . . . Rail King . . . By M. T. H. Electric Trains."

New train set accessory, in original box, by Rail King, #30-90005, box 11" x 7.25" x 3.75", c. 2000s. This standard scale railroad accessory depicts a small, stainless or aluminum trailer house, with working lights. Mobile homes are popular train set accessories. $15–$20

"Caravane Residentielle No. 370"

(Bottom) French mobile-home toy, plastic construction, by Majorette, 5.5" x 1" x 1.5", c. 1970s–1980s. This creative and scarce vintage toy incorporated several working/opening parts, including its four wheels, side entry doors, skylight, and rear picture window. Upscale toys like this one certainly contradict the trailer trash notion, and on an international level! $15–$20

More mobile home art. "Tickets . . . Closed" "Pink Trailer Tilt, Tennessee" from the "By The Way" series.

(On reverse side) Unused tourist art postcard, color photo, by Ken Brown Cards, #A97341, 5.5" x 3.5", copyright 1978. $10–$15

Picture perfect scale models!

Two train set mobile-home accessories, HO 1/87 scale, by IMEX, #6123 and #6124, c. 2000s. Notice how clean, neat, and manicured these two models depicted mobile home living. Each, $15–$20.

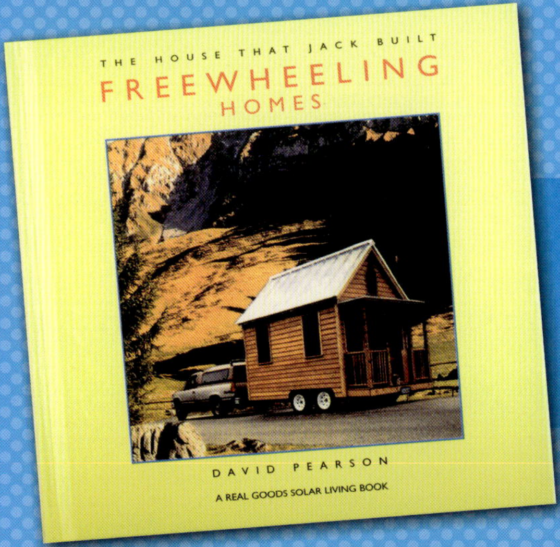

Freewheeling Homes: The House That Jack Built

Hard-cover book, color cover photo by David Pearson, 8" x 8.25", ninety-five pages, copyright 2002. This interesting little book actually explored most of the same kinds of roll-model images that we included in our first chapter, particularly the gypsy caravan and the showman's wagon. We like the tiny house shown on wheels on the book's cover. $15–$20

Big mistake! Inside Greeting: "Cake is for wimps. Happy Birthday!"

Humorous birthday greeting card, color photo, bi-fold, by Craig Orsini and Palm Press, 7" x 5" folded, 7" x 10" unfolded, copyrights 2008 and 2010. Countless mobile homes and RVs are singed, partially melted, and burned in whole or in part by careless grilling each year—especially when it is done under their patio roofs or awnings. $5–$10

"Add 80 per cent more space with Silver-Top Ranch Rooms!" (White Marsh, Maryland)

(On reverse side) Unused advertising postcard, color photo, no maker identified, unnumbered, 5.5" x 3.5", c. 1960s–1970s. Here was a stunning mobile home, sporting its impressive ranch room and awning-covered patio. $5–$10

"Modern Metal Craftsmen Inc. . . . Miami, Florida"

Unused advertising postcard, two-view, by R. C. Shaul, #24468N, 5.5" x 3.5", c. 1950s. The printed text recited: "The nationally famous Alum-O-Room Trailer Cabana and Alum-O-Roof awning are popular with trailerists everywhere." $10–$15

"18 Men On A Silver-Top Roof ..."

(On reverse side) Creative and persuasive imagery! Unused advertising postcard, color photo, by Alpert Productions, unnumbered, 5.5" x 3.5", c. 1950s–1960s. The text of the card claimed that these "awnings are built stronger to last a lifetime!" Scarce card. $10–$15

"El Cajon Awning and Manufacturing Co. . . El Cajon, California"

(On reverse side) Used advertising postcard, color photo, by H. S. Crocker, unnumbered, 5.5" x 3.5", posted 1961 from El Cajon to Lemon Grove, California. The text boasted: "The Finest Aluminum Awning for Patio, Trailer and Home." $5–$10

"This custom made sectional glass and screen Add-A-Room can be installed in varying sizes on any mobile home. . . . Hayes Equipment Co. . . . Dover, New Hampshire."

(On reverse side) Unused advertising postcard, color photo, by Tichnor Brothers, #K-16659, 5.5" x 3.5", c. 1960s–'70s. $5–$10

"Silver-Top Window Awnings... White Marsh, Md."

(On reverse side) Unused advertising postcard, color photo, by Alpert Productions, unnumbered, 5.5" x 3.5", dated 1964. $5–$10

"A beautiful Cabana like the one shown here could provide that extra space needed in your mobile home. . . . Will Mfg. Inc. . . . Calimesa, Calif."

(On reverse side) Unused advertising postcard, color photo, by Mel Lieder Photography and Dexter Press, #84988-B, 5.5" x 3.5", c. 1950s–1960s. $5–$10

"Silver-Top All-Aluminum Utility Store Rooms . . . White Marsh, Md."

(On reverse side) Unique card! Unused advertising postcard, by Dexter Press, #74014-C, 5.5" x 3.5", c. 1960s. These storage spaces are especially useful for mobile homes. $10–$15

"1973 . . . Morgan Drive Away, Inc. . . . Executive Planning Calendar" (Elkhart, Indiana)
Advertising calendar, spiral bound, twelve-month, 10" x 8", dated 1973. This company specialized in moving mobile homes and RVs. $5–$10

"Maxwell's Mobile Home Moving . . . Calmesa, Calif."
(On reverse side) Unused advertising postcard, color photo, by Thelma Kolitjoff and Dexter Press, #50393-C, 5.5" x 3.5", c. 1960s–1970s. $5–$10

"Western Trailer Supply . . . 'Mobile Home Transport Is Our Business'"
(On reverse side) Unused advertising postcard, color photo, by White and Cook, #57209, 5.5" x 3.5", c. 1950s–1960s. $5–$10

Not only trailers, but also homemade motorized vehicles (or motorhomes), were sometimes made to look like houses on wheels, as demonstrated by the vehicles on this page.

(Above) (On reverse side) "Rolling Home, Rockaway, New York, 1933" Unused reproduction postcard, black-and-white photo, by Fotofolio, #RP10, 6" x 4.25", copyright 1991. $5–$10

"Mobile Home, 1922"

(Below) (On reverse side) Unused reproduction postcard, black-and-white photo, by Pomegranate Publications, #5602, 6" x 4.25", c. 2000s. This large vehicle appeared to be some 35-40 feet in length! $5–$10

(Handwritten) "Built by W.R. Willey ..."

(Above) Unused reproduction postcard, black-and-white photo (c. 1920s–1930s), no maker identified, unnumbered, 5.5" x 3.5", c. 2000s. The primitive-looking Willey apparently lived in this homemade mobile home for a long time, as there was a reference to "22 years like this summer and winter." $5–$10

Used (but not mailed)

(Below) Tourist postcard, black-and-white photo, no maker identified, unnumbered, 5.5" x 3.5", dated 1935 (handwritten note on back). This early coach even sported a balcony at the back of the unit. Notice the couple and their dog posing for the picture. $20–$25

"Phillips 66 . . . Dealer Development"

Two used advertising postcards, one black-and-white photo, one color photo, no maker identified, unnumbered, one 5.5" x 3.25", one 5.5" x 3.5", one posted 1959 and one 1960 from Minneapolis to Rochester, Minnesota. These unusual cards were used to notify gasoline dealers where the mobile dealer development classroom would be located for dealers to attend programs to assist their gasoline businesses. $15–$20

Scarce card! "Gil Tunney's Studios, Inc. . . . York, Pennsylvania"

(On reverse side) Used advertising postcard, color photo by Gil Tunney Studios, unnumbered, 5.5" x 3.5", posted 1965 from/to York, Pennsylvania. Called the "Photo Rover," the pictured house trailer was a unique mobile photography studio. $10–$15

Red on red! "Mobile Office Inc . . . 36 Ft. Air-Conditioned Field Office . . . Chicago, Illinois"

Unused advertising postcard, color photo, by Curteichcolor, #4C-K1471, 5.5" x 3.5", c. 1950s–1960s. Rare card! $15–$20

"Chez Charlot . . . Rimouski, Quebec" (Canada)

(On reverse side) Unused advertising postcard, color photo, by UNIC and Studio Bernard, #45275-B, 5.5" x 3.5", c. 1970s–'80s. What a bright and handsome vintage diner this mobile provided! $15–$20

Bibliography

Barber, Nicola. *Mobile Home: Homes Around the World.* East Sussex, England: Wayland Ltd., 2006.

Clark, Martin. *The Many Aspects of Mobile Home Living* (Novel). New York: Alfred Knopf, 2000.

Foxworthy, Jeff. *Redneck Extreme Mobile Home Makeover*. Nashville: Rutledge Hill Press, 2005.

Gillespie, Hollis. *Trailer Trashed: My Dubious Efforts Toward Upward Mobility.* Guilford, CT: Globe Pequot Press, 2008.

Keister, Douglas. *Mobile Mansions: Taking "Home Sweet Home" on the Road*. Salt Lake City, UT: Gibbs Smith, 2006.

Nappo, Donatto, and Stefania Vairelli. *Homes on the Move: Mobile Architecture*. Konigswinter, Germany: H.F. Ullmann, 2010.

Nulsen, Robert. *All About Parks for Mobile Homes and Trailers.* Beverly Hills: Trail-R-Club of America, 1968.

Pearson, David. *Freewheeling Homes: The House That Jack Built*. White River Junction, VT: Chelsea Green, 2002.

Rickard, Graham. *Mobile Homes.* East Sussex, England: Wayland Ltd., 1988.

Wallis, Allan. *Wheel Estate: The Rise and Decline of Mobile Homes.* Baltimore: Johns Hopkins University Press, 1991.

Acknowledgments

To our very talented Schiffer Publishing editor Dinah Roseberry and designer Matt Goodman.

Our most sincere thanks to all the exceptional editors and designers at Schiffer Publishing for their capable guidance provided in the course of this book's production. This is our eighth book with Schiffer, and we feel blessed to have gained the confidence and to have the support of such an outstanding publishing house.

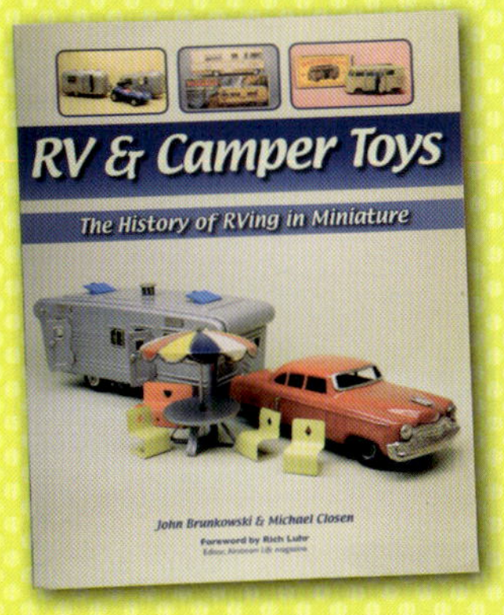

RV and Camper Toys: The History of RVing in Miniature

Coffee-table style, 375 color photos of more than 800 collectible pieces, 126 page book, authors John Brunkowski and Michael Closen, by Iconographix Inc., copyright 2008. The only book ever written about RV toys, including trailer house and mobile home toys. $25–$30.

The Long, Long Trailer

DVD cover graphic, for the 1954 MGM film, starring Lucille Ball and Desi Arnaz, copyright 2006. This sixty-year-old movie, which is still popular today, is the all-time classic mobile-home film, featuring a forty-foot-long state-of-the-art trailer house of its time. In spite of all the problems and mishaps encountered by Lucy and Desi in their trailer, this internationally acclaimed movie provided a highly positive impression about mobile home living. For the DVD, $10–$15.

Other Schiffer Books by the Authors

KOA and the Art of Kamping
ISBN: 978-0-7643-4520-3

Airstream Memories
ISBN: 978-0-7643-4163-2

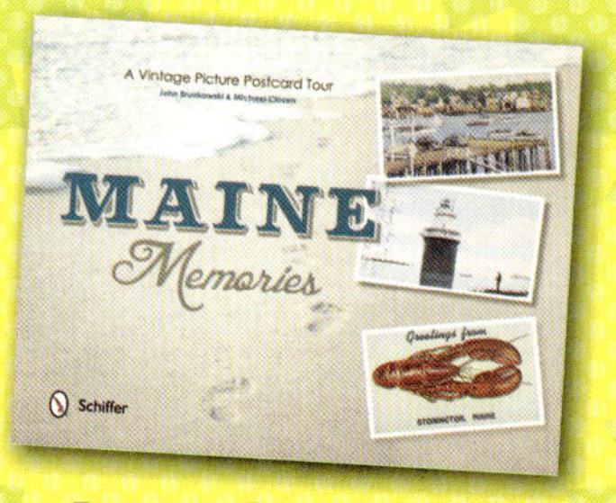

Maine Memories
A Vintage Picture Postcard Tour
ISBN: 978-0-7643-4846-4

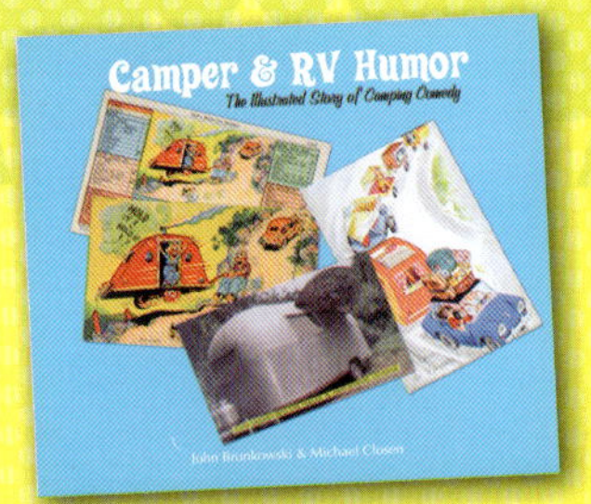

Camper and RV Humor
The Illustrated Story of Camping Comedy
ISBN: 978-0-7643-4705-4

Amateur Radio Goes Camping and RVing
The Illustrated QSL Card History
ISBN: 978-0-7643-4529-6

Pictorial Guide to RVing
ISBN: 978-0-7643-3546-4

Gift and Shopping Bag Designs
ISBN: 978-0-7643-4969-0